Developmental
MANAGEMENT

CONCEPTUAL TOOLMAKING

D0542428

Developmental Management

General Editor: Ronnie Lessem

Charting the Corporate Mind
*Charles Hampden-Turner**

Managing in the Information Society
Yoneji Masuda

Developmental Management
Ronnie Lessem

Foundations of Business
Ivan Alexander

Ford on Management
*Henry Ford**

Managing the Developing Organization
Bernard Lievegoed

Managing Your Self
Jagdish Parikh

Greening Business
John Davis

Conceptual Toolmaking
Jerry Rhodes

* For copyright reasons this edition is not available in the USA

Conceptual Toolmaking

EXPERT SYSTEMS OF THE MIND

JERRY RHODES

WITH A FOREWORD BY
RONNIE LESSEM

Copyright © Jerry Rhodes 1991, 1994
Foreword © Ronnie Lessem 1991, 1994

The right of Jerry Rhodes to be identified as author of this work has been asserted in accordance with the Copyright, Designs and Patents Act 1988.

First published 1991
First published in paperback 1994
Reprinted 1994

Blackwell Publishers
108 Cowley Road
Oxford OX4 1JF
UK

238 Main Street
Cambridge, Massachusetts 02142
USA

British Library Cataloguing in Publication Data

A CIP catalogue record for this book is available from the British Library.

Library of Congress Cataloging in Publication Data

A CIP catalogue record for this book is available from the Library of Congress.

ISBN 0–631–17489–3
ISBN 0–631–19321–9 (paper)

Typeset in 11 on 13 pt Ehrhardt
by Hope Services (Abingdon) Ltd.
Printed in Great Britain by
T.J. Press Ltd., Padstow, Cornwall.

This book is printed on acid-free paper.

Contents

Foreword: Management Thinking

by Ronnie Lessem

Introduction

Jerry Rhodes' book on Conceptual Toolmaking is a true rarity in management circles in that it represents the culmination of a programme of research and development that has spanned over fifteen years.

Unlike research and development in the physical sciences, which business has espoused for well over a century, there is no established tradition of such business-sponsored R & D in the social sciences. It is therefore of special interest to us that Philips in Holland took the lead, in the seventies and eighties, in promoting fundamental research into managerial thinking. Although a whole team of researchers, in Europe, participated in the research programme, it is Jerry Rhodes who has done the most to collate and disseminate the results of this unique work.

Rhodes, an Oxford graduate with a scientific bent, comes from a highly artistic family in Great Britain, and has been a gifted athlete, a Hoover salesman, an executive at Rank Xerox, as well as a distinguished management consultant in his lifetime. His previous book, *The Colours of your Mind*[1], has established Rhodes' credentials as perhaps the leading representative of a very distinguished British school of management thought.

Because the British are well known for hiding their light under a bushel they have failed to establish themselves, as the Americans have done, as a conceptual force to be reckoned with in management. This is particularly unfortunate because, by virtue of the English language, the British have been in a leading position to champion a European, alongside an American or now Japanese, approach to management theory and practice. In fact, seen through an alien pair of eyes like my own, it is quite evident that such a distinctive approach does exist. It comes under the guise of *management learning and development* into which Rhodes' work can be comfortably positioned. The elder statesman in this learner-centred approach to management is the physicist Reg Revans; probably its most ingenious exponent is the computer scientist Stafford Beer; the best known such management thinker is the kidney specialist Edward de Bono; and Jerry Rhodes is the most recent to emerge in such an eminent line of gifted British amateurs!

Action Learning

The Springs of Human Action

Reg Revans, like Jerry Rhodes, was a great athlete in his youth, and a Cambridge physicist, that is before he turned his heart and mind – in the 1940s – to professional and management education. Revans, in fact, first turned his attention to the problems of raising productivity among hospital nurses and coalminers. In the forty years that have followed, Revans' concept of 'action learning', which we shall soon uncover, has been applied to public and private enterprises in America and in Australia, in Bangladesh and in Belgium, in Egypt and in the Republic of Ireland, and only scantily in the United Kingdom.

Revans is a scientist, first and foremost, who is interested in the way that individuals and organizations learn from their experiences. For him, management science is much more concerned with the 'springs of human action' than it is with particular methods of work study or with managerial problem solving. In that respect Revans draws on the interactive and imaginative Celtic strain of European thought rather than the active and methodical Teutonic one.

It is one's perception of the problem, one's evaluation of what is to be gained by solving it and one's estimate of the resources at hand to solve it that together provide the springs of human action. Since these judgments are largely those of one's relations to others, and since at the present rate of technological change the problems to be solved differ from one day to the next, it follows that everybody in the organization, from those who frame the policies to those who manipulate the ultimate details of technique, must be endowed to the greatest possible extent with the means of learning.[2]

In the fifties and sixties Revans studied the attitudes and performance of people in scores of factories, mines, schools and hospitals in Britain. What he found was that the quality of information that individuals had at their disposal was the most important determinant of positive attitude and effective performance. The quality of information, in fact, was heavily influenced by its accessibility, so that the scale of organization had an important part to play. In that respect, even if for somewhat different reasons, Revans was led to similar conclusions to his European contemporary, Fritz Schumacher, that is to say that *Small is Beautiful*.[3]

Human beings learn only when they want to learn, and only when they identify themselves with persons from whom, or for whom, they want to do so. In the big organization, this personal identification is always difficult. Since most men, having lived with themselves for a lifetime, have ceased to reflect much on anything so familiar as their own self image, it is hard for them to understand their relations with others, especially from a distance.[4]

Learning must be Greater than the Rate of Change

At the centre of Revans' world-view, then, as for Jerry Rhodes, lies neither management nor organization – as is the case for the conventionally rational manager – but individual, organizational and societal learning. Those who cannot keep up with what is new will lose control of their surroundings, while those who take change in their stride will profit by being able to turn it to their advantage.

In the final analysis, then, learning must be greater than the rate of change. Moreover, and this is crucial to Revans' argument, you cannot change the system of which you are in command, at least in any new sense, unless you are yourself changed in the process – since the logical structure of both are in correspondence. In other words, for Revans, the underlying structures of successful achievement, of learning and of intelligent counselling, and of what we call scientific method, are logically identical.

I locate the manager, as the individual he is and must always remain, at the centre of the activity that engages him. A real decision, firstly, is always that of a particular person, with his own ends not to be neglected, his own fears to amplify his problems, his own hopes a mirage to magnify his resources, and his own prejudices, often called experience, to colour the data in which he works. A choice of goals, secondly, so much bound up with decision theory, is yet distinct from it, in that the ends for which one strives, deliberately or subconsciously, as an individual or with others, are but partly determined by the calculations of economic strategy; behind them jostle the egocentric drives of the individual. Thirdly, information is a product of which the raw material is data and the manufacturing process the sensitivities of the individual. Fourthly, the theory of systems describes the web in which the world-line of a particular manager is entangled. The assessment of probability is, fifthly, the farrago of mathematical statistics and simple guesswork by which we attempt to assess our forgotten experience, our present wishfulness and our future hope. And, sixthly, the learning process integrates everything that one has so far become, and one's sole hope for future improvement.[5]

Managing Learning; Learning Managing

Management and learning, for Revans as for Rhodes, for Edward de Bono as for Stafford Beer, are intimately interconnected. Both are intrinsically concerned with the processing of information and with the resolution of complex problems. In fact Revans characterizes management in terms of three systems based on the use of information: system alpha, the use of information for designing objectives; system beta, the use of information for achieving these objectives; and system gamma, the use of information for adapting to experience and change.

System Alpha

System alpha, then, is a personalized version of a corporate strategy. A course of action, Revans maintains, in order for it to be flexible, demands of a manager that he value what he anticipates will be its outcome; second, the manager must be aware of the external difficulties he will need to surmount in order to achieve his intended result; and third, he needs to find internal resources enough to deal with these difficulties at a cost consonant with the value of the outcome.

System Beta

Whereas system alpha is involved with designing objectives, or strategy, system beta is concerned with achieving them. It is scientific method in personal and organizational motion. It is a system for both constructive learning and for effective action. It involves, all in all, five elements within an integrated process. Survey, stage one, involves observation and information gathering. Hypothesis, stage two, involves inference, conjecture, theorizing. Experiment, stage three, involves the carrying out of a series of practical tests. Inspection, stage four, engages the learner and manager in comparing actual against desired results. Finally, stage five, control and delegation, relates the particular and personal result to the general and organizational context.

System Gamma

System gamma, finally, brings the individual learner back into the picture. As a particular person, he confronts a problem in a unique way and takes in the facts according to his 'predisposing mental set'. For it is his personal values, combined with the external problem and the internal resources, which condition both his decision and his learning. In adapting himself to experience and change he must combine objective science with subjective values. Learning, then, involves subjective motive as well as objective method.

The Cardinal Postulates of Action Learning

It took some twenty-five years for Revans to come up with a precise methodology for action learning. In the early seventies he began to arrive at his great synthesis, which he has been refining ever since. Here are what might be termed his cardinal postulates:

- Learning is a function of programmed knowledge (P) and questioning insight (Q). Questioning insight involves knowing the right questions to ask in conditions of ignorance and uncertainty.

- When the world does not change, the son may follow the father's footsteps, and programmed knowledge is sufficient. But, at the precipice, when you are climbing into a new world at every step, the primary need is for questioning insight.

- You cannot change the system of which you are in command, fundamentally, unless you are changed in the process. The first change Revans calls action and the second learning.

- The theory of learning, whose inner logic corresponds with scientific method, suggests that the recognition of one's need to learn, the search for new knowledge, the test of that new knowledge in practical action, the critical evaluation of the results of that test, and the consolidation of the whole exercise in memory, are all essential to complete learning.

- Those best able to help in developing the self are comrades in adversity who also struggle to understand themselves; you lose the dread of going into your own chamber of horrors, Revans suggests, when you find yourself opening the doors for others to face what might be lurking in their own.

- Organizations best able to develop themselves are those which make better use of their existing resources because a social process of learning has been engendered within them. That process is calculated to help them identify internal strengths and weaknesses, to understand better their inertias and dynamics, and in other ways to make more use of their shared experiences.

- Individual and organizational learning, development and problem solving are all manifestations of the same process. In both microcosm and macrocosm:

  > learning must imply the power to perform the action as well as to specify it;
  >
  > people and organizations learn, or change their behaviour in a real way, of their own volition and not at the will of others;
  >
  > in learning such behaviour people must attack real problems; and so as to be aware of their real progress these attacks must carry significant risk of penalty for failure;
  >
  > continuous comparison between prediction and outcome of results will bring home to the person or enterprise the nature of their learning;
  >
  > the deliberate analysis and modification of a real life problem uses the scientific method and thus reflects the learning process of all who take part.

Revans, then, viewed scientific method (system beta) and learning as parallel processes. As such a scientist he has followed a long-standing and fertile European tradition. In action and in experimentation lies freedom; in reflection and in conceptualization lies order. Action learning combined dissolves this polarity.

The scientific and industrial revolution emerged from a Europe that was emancipating itself from religious dogma. Through science a new way was discovered of combining freedom of thought with an orderly pursuit of knowledge. The learning achieved, through a conscious and orderly attempt to get to grips with business and management problems is not so much an acquaintance with factual or technical art by some authority. Rather it involves the reinterpretation of the subject's existing knowledge, including his recollection of past lived experiences.

The continuous process of liberating our minds from the programs implanted in our brains is a prerequisite of personal evolution. We can embark on that process of liberation only by constantly and consciously testing the ways in which our personal variety has been and is being constrained by the very things we hold dear.[6]

Design for Freedom

Variety absorbs Variety

This call for the accommodation of personal and organizational variety has been continually made by an illustrious colleague of Revans, Stafford Beer, who was president of the International Society for Operations Research in the sixties. Beer is a brilliant computer scientist who has worked with corporations and governments around the world to make the most imaginative use of management science and of their computer-based resources.

In the 1940s, both in Europe and America, operations research (OR) was born. Arising out of the application of mathematical and statistical techniques to the solving of technical and logistical problems of warfare, a 'management science' was created. Since that time Stafford Beer has become increasingly concerned that this so-called 'science' was being used to narrow management's options rather than to broaden them.

Our culture insists on the uniqueness of the individual, but our society cannot live up to that. Instead of understanding the situation, and using science to do the best possible job of variety attenuation under the guidance of the consumer and the electorate, we spend vast sums of national wealth on phoney claims.[7]

Beer has continually maintained that in order to regulate a system we have to absorb its variety. If we fail in this the system becomes unstable. Variety absorbs variety and nothing else can. The manager able to absorb such variety is *homo gubernator*, man the steersman, steering between freedom and order, surrounded by large, complex and interactive systems.

Beer compares and contrasts, then, *homo gubernator* with *homo faber*. *Homo faber*, he says, is out of date. Man, at least in industrialized societies, is no longer threatened by the cold and by wild animals. He is threatened by exploding complexity. For the new manager-steersman information rather than energy is the key raw material.

The stuff of information and control is variety. Variety is defined by Beer as the number of possible states of a system. In a totalitarian regime that variety is severely constrained, whereas in a democracy many more possible varieties of behaviour are possible and desirable. Therein lies the rub. The management problem in a 'free' organization is precisely that of handling variety. The more individuality the *gubernator* accommodates the greater the complexity of the human system with which he is dealing. Management must therefore be capable of generating as much control variety as the situation is capable of generating uncontrolled variety.

The Brain of the Firm

The full-scale handling of variety is completely impossible for the brain of man. Traditionally, because of man's limited capacities, the approach has been to chop down variety on a mammoth scale. The form and function of autocracy or bureaucracy is what has resulted. Think about the history of management. The origins of large-scale modern enterprises were in small companies controlled often by autocratic entrepreneurs, and these men did everything that mattered themselves. Those that worked for them followed a leader and did what they were told. Small firms to this day often begin like this, recapitulating a development scheme that was common at the time of the industrial revolution. When the firm grows larger the boss is compelled to delegate or bust. Now it is natural, according to Stafford Beer, that in these circumstances a man should delegate the things he least likes doing. That leads to an arbitrary form of organization, especially once it becomes depersonalized.

Now if arbitrariness is the first reason why we might object to this orthodoxy, Beer argues, the second is much more powerful. It is that there exists today a power to cope with information vastly in excess of human capacity, with the result that the manager is no longer the arbiter of sophistication in control. Rather he has to organize the firm so that it can be computed with in such a way that the surrounding complexity can be appropriately handled. Therefore if he asks the question 'how can I make the best use of computers in my business?' he is asking the wrong question. He should be investigating how his business should be run, given that the computers exist.[8]

Stafford Beer, over the past thirty years, has written some two hundred articles and six original books, to help politicians and managers to cope with complexity. He has been a consultant to the UN, to NATO, to European and American governments and corporations. He has also painted pictures and written poetry. His versatility, in that respect, is matched by that of his well known colleague, Edward de Bono.

Lateral Thinking

The New Renaissance

In the same way as Reg Revans was trained as a physicist, and Stafford Beer as a mathematician, so Edward de Bono was originally trained to be a medical doctor. Since that time he has been responsible for the establishment of a Ministry of Intelligence in Venezuela, for the teaching of thinking skills in schools around the world, and for the training of thousands of managers in his so-called 'lateral thinking'. Evidently the cult of the gifted amateur still thrives in Great Britain.

In his latest, and twentieth book on thinking, entitled *I am Right – You are Wrong*, de Bono has heralded the coming of a new renaissance.

The last Renaissance was clearly based on the rediscovery of ancient Greek (about 400 BC) thinking habits of logic, reason, argument, truth and the importance of man. Before the last Renaissance the thinking habits of the Western world were derived entirely from dogma and theology . . . The search for truth – as distinct from dogma – was to be made through the exposure of falsity by means of argument, reason and logic. This reason, not dogma was to decide what was right and wrong. We can be duly appreciative of our traditional thinking culture and also realize that it is inadequate. It may have been adequate for the period in which it was developed (ancient Greece and medieval Europe) but at that time there were stable societies, agreed perceptions and limited technical change. Today there are problems caused by rapidly accelerating change.[9]

In the new renaissance that de Bono believes we are entering we need to shift, he says, from cleverness to wisdom. Analysis has its place but there is a need for constructive design. 'I do not believe that we should abandon the use of the most excellent resource; the human mind and its thinking. Instead we should aim to develop thinking habits that are more constructive and more creative than we now have.'[10]

These new thinking habits are to be modelled on the pattern-making and self-organizing capacities of the human brain which, for the first time in the eighties and nineties, can be simulated with some degree of accuracy. In fact some twenty years ago de Bono first pointed out this pattern-making nature of the human brain. This led him, in turn, to place great emphasis on the self-organizing powers of human perception in general, and of lateral thinking in particular.

Vertical and Lateral Thinking

de Bono likens logic to vertical thinking and perception to lateral thinking.[11] Whereas, for him:

- vertical thinking is *selective*, lateral thinking is *generative*;
- vertical thinking moves only if there is a direction in which to move, lateral thinking moves in order to generate a direction;
- vertical thinking is *analytical*, lateral thinking is *provocative*;
- vertical thinking is *sequential*, lateral thinking makes *jumps*;
- with vertical thinking one has to be correct at every step, whereas with lateral thinking one does not have to be;
- with vertical thinking one concentrates and *excludes* what is irrelevant, whereas with lateral thinking one welcomes *chance intrusions*;
- vertical thinking follows the most likely paths and lateral thinking the least likely;
- vertical thinking is a *finite* process, whereas lateral thinking is a *probabilistic* one.

de Bono has argued, continually, that to the extent that we become exclusively vertical thinkers so we become locked into structures that inhibit our freedom of action. In practice these structures are the institutions we have and, even more importantly, the concepts and habits of thinking that structure our mind. Thinking, in its fullest sense, is the tool with which man appreciates, explores and changes not only the outer world, through his plans and actions, but also his inner world. Like Revans, de Bono maintains that to change a system, out there, in any significant way, you need to first change yourself.

Conclusion

Jerry Rhodes – like Reg Revans, Stafford Beer and Edward de Bono – is a gifted amateur in the best of British traditions. He trained to be a schoolmaster and ended up as a management consultant. More importantly, however, he is the most recent and arguably the most coherent advocate of conceptual toolmaking as the key to open the door to effective management in an increasingly complex world.

Whereas the Japanese and the Germans have become the most proficient craftsmen, engineers and machine toolmakers of our modern era it may well be that the British, probably together with the French, will become the most effective conceptual toolmakers. 'The ability to make his own tools is one of the hallmarks of a master craftsman: it distinguishes him', Rhodes says, 'from the majority of those who are less professional. The manager of complex change who is at a premium today needs to be a toolmaker too – only his tools are primarily to do with mental rather than physical skill.'

The more senior the manager, Rhodes argues from both knowledge and experience, the more he or she needs to rely on mental process rather than mere stock of knowledge.

Similarly, the greater the degree of change, the more he or she needs to rely on questioning insight (to use Revans' phrase) rather than programmed knowledge. The manager advances from *homo faber*, man the maker, to *homo gubernator*.

While Jerry Rhodes draws implicitly if not explicitly on his illustrious predecessors – Revans, Beer and de Bono – he has gone further than any of them to develop a versatile technology, or thinking map, for the conceptual manager. In that respect, whereas he may lack the epic turn of phrase of Reg Revans, the eccentricity of a Stafford Beer, or the populist touch of Edward de Bono, he is ultimately the most thorough, well-researched and well-disciplined of the British school. As I have already indicated, he has researched and developed his approach systematically, and in association with a multinational corporation, Philips in Holland, over the past fifteen years. Through this book we can now benefit from their combined mental process and experience.

Notes

1 Rhodes, J. and Thame S., *The Colours of Your Mind*. Fontana, London, 1989.
2 Revans, R., 'Linking artisan and scribe' *New Society*, June 1964.
3 Schumacher, E., *Small is Beautiful*. Abacus, Tunbridge Wells, 1973.
4 Revans, R., *Developing Effective Managers*, Longman, London, 1974.
5 Revans, *Developing Effective Managers*, 1974.
6 Beer, S., *Design for Freedom*, Prentice Hall, Englewood Cliffs, NJ, 1974.
7 Beer, *Design for Freedom*, 1974.
8 Beer, S., *Platform for Change*, Wiley, Chichester, 1975.
9 de Bono, E., *I Am Right – You Are Wrong*, Viking, London, 1990.
10 de Bono, *I Am Right – You Are Wrong*, 1990.
11 de Bono, *Lateral Thinking for Management*, Penguin, Harmondsworth, 1982.

Preface

A book creates a world of its own, the reader an active player in the creation. On reading through and reflecting on the chapters I realize that while they invite the reader to be intelligently active they also demonstrate why conceptual tools are so much needed. The very subject of thinking about thinking is just about the toughest area of education and development. It is essentially abstract and extremely unforgiving. It is the cool core of behaviour. The limits to intellectual endurance are quickly reached and most people will find themselves likely to exclaim 'My brain is hurting'.

This is just why tools are needed for concepts. What takes many pages to spell out can be shown almost in a flash. The whole idea of the conceptual tool is to represent great complexity in simple form. Thus it can be grasped, accessed and remembered very fast indeed. To take advantage of this compression and the many different uses for each tool it's best of course for someone to be shown a tool live. Then he has an immediate sense of how it works and can try it out with the person handing it on to him. Reading about a tool is one thing, but grasping hold of it and producing results from using it is the best way to understand and gain value from it. Because any tool springs to life only in the hand of a person, you need the real situations facing you to feel the living force of these conceptual tools. Nonetheless, it is the idea of conceptual toolmaking that this book is advancing, not the practical application or the depth of detail which can only be gained with experience at first hand. What I realize now is that the very practical nature of the tools you will find in these pages makes it a paradox to write about them.

Reviewers and publicists are apt to ask authors 'How sexy is it?' even when the topic falls into the serious business of thinking for business. This book's title with the word 'conceptual' figuring so boldly might suggest it is not sexy at all. My wife, Sue Thame, who was once a journalist, was told in her salad days that she would never make a sub-editor because she missed all the innuendos. In subbing this book she has been only too alert to them. A 'tool' stirs earthy allusions. We both hope that an image here or there occasionally triggers a mischievous twinkle. In preparing the final manuscript we spent a delightful month which Sue described as 'conceptual lovemaking'. Perhaps that should have been the title!

I deliberately chose the dissonance of the actual title, mixing the cerebral with the physical, to express the paradox of the message of this book. My abiding memory of a first-rate craftsman I worked with in GKN was that he was always banging on that toolmakers were the highest skilled workers of the lot. His insistence obviously stuck because now I am an enthusiast for the art and science of toolmaking. Interestingly this man, John Bone, became a training instructor, identifying the conceptual components of his practical skills and embodying them in visible and tangible teaching methods, in order to pass his expertise on to others. He was a conceptual toolmaker as well. No wonder he was soon on his way up the management pyramid. We need to grow more of this kind of skilful thinker; one who can not only 'do' a good job but can also understand and communicate how he does it. The pace of change demands constant learning which in turn is based on thinking about thinking. Can we also raise our conceptual sights to operate our organizations this way?

All writers today encounter the hazard of the third person pronoun. I have followed the custom and practice with which I am familiar, and embraced male and female within 'he'. I have my wife's assurance that I am not a male chauvinist, but recognize that if you do not agree with this convention it can appear relentlessly masculine. Yet the insistence on his/her or (s)he can be not only cumbersome but actively irritating to the poor old reader. So I can only hope that those who might otherwise be affronted will recognize that my intentions are honourable.

Another style idiosyncrasy is forced by the spelling of just three jargon words, namely Realise, Categorise and Symbolise, with the 's' instead of the Blackwell house-style of 'z'.

The book is intended for everyone with an interest in improving the results obtained from thinking, most especially in business. This includes public services as well as commerce and industry. I often refer to 'managers' and it might appear that I am implying that only managers need to think. My use of the word is a shorthand not only for those who manage mainstream operations, but also specialists and professionals, and those senior people whose contribution is to think beyond the current operation and determine the very direction of the business. But high or low, those whose jobs depend on their ability to think well have to manage their minds, and thus I see them as managers.

Although it appears first, this preface is the last to be written, so it enables me to see the book in perspective, after the nitty-gritty of putting one word after another. It is not an academic treatise, so it is not referenced with sources, mainly because I cannot remember all the wonderful work other people have done which has influenced my thinking. Academics usually only acknowledge what has been published, but most of my learning has been from real live people like John Bone.

If I were to advance a criticism of my own work here it would be that perhaps I have devoted too much to description and not enough to persuasion. My defence would be that it is more important first to describe what is as yet not well known. This has ever been an issue for me. Publishers, though thankfully not this one, like simple stories of success to lard their books. It has not been my experience that you can put success down to one key factor – in particular the intervention of one's own methods. Too many contingencies impact any human situation. I dislike the shallow promotion that proclaims 'This is the answer to. . .'. What I have tried to do is fill the book with practical illustrations of the tools I am describing, giving you the reader enough substance to pursue the ideas yourself and test them for their value.

This is the second book I have written and once again it is my family who has given me the greatest support, especially during these last months when I have retreated from social contact in order to deliver the manuscript on time. While I have nursed it along my elder daughter has been nursing her first child. For the newest generation who will become conceptual thinkers of a high order, I dedicate this book to Emily Louise.

Jerry Rhodes

Jerry Rhodes
Cotswold House
16 Bradley Street
Wotton-under-Edge
Gloucestershire GL12 7AR
Tel (01453) 521585 Fax 521686

Acknowledgements

I would like to offer some recognition for all those from whom I have learned something that has gone into this book. When it comes to its faults and shortcomings, those should not be placed on any shoulders but my own.

Even if I do not name individual people, I must at least mention those organizations that have given me my opportunities for learning about conceptual toolmaking. I have been paid for bringing my know-how to them, but at the same time I have always brought away contributions from them. In some cases, their contribution stemmed mainly from asking me to run a management development programme for them in-house, and working with me on its design or execution and at best with its follow-up. In a few cases, joint development projects with them have been sustained over many years and then the client contribution has been truly substantial. For example, Figure 3.2 and 7.1 were developed with Philips and, notably, the Thunks themselves. To all of these organizations I offer my acknowledgement and thanks.

Banking
Allied Irish Bank
Barclays Bank
National Westminster Bank
Royal Bank of Scotland
T S B

Other Financial Services
Abbey Life
Allied Dunbar
Deloitte
Dun & Bradstreet
English & American
London Life
Manulife

Oil and Chemicals
Esso
Kalle-Duphar
Hoechst
Shell

Electronics and Information
I C L
Marconi
Philips
Rank Xerox
Thorn
Wang

Manufacturing
Alfa Laval
Austin Rover
Dunlop
Ingersoll Engineers
Kimberly Clark
United Biscuits

Public Sector and Utilities
Aston University
British Coal
British Gas
British Rail
British Steel
Central Electricity Generating Board
Jutland Technology Institute
Public Service Training Council

Others
Celmi
British Junior Chamber of Commerce
Centre for the Study of Management Learning
Granard Rowland

I

The Conceptual Manager

As you open this book you must be wondering what you expect to find. What on earth is conceptual toolmaking? If you are a manager with experience and success behind you the odds are that you will see conceptual about as far from toolmaking as can be. Many people think the first to be about abstract theory and the second about practical action and, for too many, one has nothing to do with the other. Such a view may be understandable but when the chips are down it is arrant nonsense. Anyone with an ounce of sense knows there is a difference between theory that is pure speculation, an hypothesis, and theory that is formed from the analysis of experience. What you do with speculation is to test it before placing your trust in it: the more severe the testing, the greater your confidence if it survives. But to sheer away from theory that is founded on success is in plain terms to court failure. Theory of this kind not only works, but saves work. It becomes a kind of tool.

This book is about the making of conceptual tools. The concept is used not only as a metaphor but as a literal description – even conceptual tools can be given physical form. But they have a high know-how content, and the know-how they reflect can stretch to a rather high order of abstraction. Yet although they come from a specialist base, they are more and more needed by the generalist manager and even by everyone who depends on his or her skill in using information to get results. Some areas of human activity can still be handled well with long-established and unchanging tools that have been developed over many years of doing roughly the same thing over and over again, like accounting and auditing. More and more people now however are finding themselves facing up to situations they have never dealt with before. Old recipes don't seem to fit. All those managers who can no longer depend on referring to 'how it was done before' need to be independent of personal experience, and need to make their own tools for each situation. It is to these people that this book is especially addressed. The ability to make his own tools is one of the hallmarks of a master craftsman: it distinguishes him from the majority of those who are less professional. Managers of complex change who are at a premium today need to be toolmakers too – only their tools are primarily to do with mental rather than physical skill. Those tools form a special kind of know-how.

Who doesn't believe in know-how? Managers and experts of all kinds, sportsmen and performers, farmers and seafarers, artists and poets, everyone has his own idea of what this means to him. It is the treasured area that reflects all the wisdom and experience of a profession. Some will claim that their special know-how is ineffable and shroud it all in mystique; others guard it jealously as the key to their competitive advantage. Harder to recognize is what could be called the know-how of know-how. Like philosophy this is central to our life but rather unknowable. If it can be reached, it offers the pass key to whatever is common to all the diverse areas of expertise. The only way to reach such know-how is by abstraction in a big way. This is central to what I mean by conceptualizing, a lever to move the world.

As you have picked up this book I can assume you believe in the value of thinking more than most. My purpose is to explore how to raise its quality through conceptual toolmaking. It is a divine irony and paradox that those who have the least need for it are the most likely to want to raise their game. Because they are already well above average, they have the nous to see how much better they could be, and the motive force to pursue the possibility. At least this is my hunch, based upon more than twenty years of working with high-potential managers, helping them to develop their conceptual powers. So this book does not set out to be a cookbook of good practice for novices, but something which could enter like fire into the soul of the most able and experienced people.

First I had better make clear that I have not found conceptual skill to be the only mark of the effective person: far from it. If I had to pick just three yardsticks for measuring the manager of the future they would be these: market awareness, skill with people and conceptual power. Acknowledging the importance of the first two, this book will focus on the third. Lack of conceptual power certainly puts limits on success in the other two areas.

Conceptualizing is surely the art of the future: not only the skill that managers will need in future, but the skill of handling the future itself. Our world has become both global and small, because our technology has made it possible for us to communicate from our living rooms with every form of art and science, business and culture, through books, newspapers, radio, television, electronic networking, telephones, computer conferencing and so on. A corporate manager is informed not just by the computer on his desk, the business meetings he attends, the financial journals he reads, the training programmes he joins, or even the lunches with his colleagues. The whole of his life, whether it be hobbies, holidays, friends, charitable interests, his children's schooling, theatre outings, gardening or love of art and music, informs his business decisions.

Every person's work is inextricably linked into everything else. We are all a part of each other in every aspect of life. Politics is not separated from art, nor science from animal husbandry, neither is education from manufacturing, nor religion from economics. I cannot sleep untroubled while millions endure famine and displacement from their homes and while other millions lay waste their precious resources. The only way to draw together the links that will ensure our survival ecologically, system-wide, so that all the richness and variegated delights of human civilizations can continue to develop, is by thinking better.

Whereas many managers believe they have to choose between thinking and action and feel drawn to 'where the action is', I hold strongly that thinking is not only a rehearsal for action: it is itself a form of action. You think when you want to get a result which is better than whatever would happen without it. Thinking back over past events is done mainly with future action in mind. All thinking aims to be either a faster, less risky or more efficient activity than doing, otherwise why waste energy on it? Yet there is a die-hard attitude that still survives in many managers that thinking smells of the abstract and must be the enemy of action. There are in fact many leaders who would be loath to recognize themselves in the role of conceptual leader. If I describe managers in this way to their face they look aghast or slightly amused, until their curiosity pushes them to question what on earth I mean.

Even George Bush, in the speech he made at the end of his

honeymoon 100 days as new President of the United States of America, was heard to say, 'I'm a practical man. I don't deal in airy abstractions.' I wonder whether he said this to be populist or because he actually believes it. It is certainly in the Anglo-Saxon/American tradition to appear to scorn too much intelligence. It was Henry Ford who so roundly declared that 'History is bunk', though he spent a lifetime making it. Those who are loudest in their dismissal of abstraction are the very people that have made their fortune out of it. Leaders in business and world affairs succeed or fail on the quality of the abstractions they make, far more than any supposed role as 'action man'. The dichotomy between action and abstraction is a delusion.

What is the Conceptual Manager?

Over the past two generations we have seen all manner of images for the perfect manager. Each has placed emphasis on something seen as being at the core of effectiveness. We have had the rational, the analytic, the bureaucratic manager; the realist and the pragmatic manager; the sensitive motivator and the controlling autocrat; the charismatic, and the inspirational visionary; the entrepreneur and the creative manager. The role of the manager is certainly that of an all-rounder and it is small wonder that there are more descriptions of his task than there are even for 'leadership'. Yet most people would agree that he is someone responsible for somehow getting results; that he mostly gets these through other people; and that he tries to get the right things done right. What is significant by its absence in all the descriptions of managers is that to do all these things in a maelstrom of uncertainty and change demands constant and rapid conceptualizing. It is this insight that is causing so many leading organizations to recognize that all their managers need to be alert learners at all times. So much is new that it needs to be conceptualized fast. You can't mess about or an opportunity will be lost or a threat will overtake you.

Mental Process

What do I mean, then, by conceptual? It is their *mental process* that distinguishes effective managers, leaders of commerce, industry, art, science, religion, education, health, government. It can still be the case that sometimes they also *know* more than others. But this dependence on knowledge and experience is rapidly diminishing. When I was born everything depended on what you knew. Halfway through my life it's all changed. As change in almost every field accelerates, knowledge and experience can be relied on less and less, because it is either impossible to get enough of it or it becomes out of date. It might even be a disadvantage at times. Mental processes, rather than data, enable conceptual leaders to be effective, helping them to pre-select in advance, identifying what will matter to them, what will be relevant even when apparently remote. They can sift things that belong together, distinguish between things that seem similar, see the causal connection between separated events, and so on. The more senior the job the more reliance on mental process and the less on detailed knowledge. Likewise, the greater the degree of change, the more reliance on a process for asking questions, and the less on the experience available for the answers. When everything is changing so rapidly and significantly, old experience diminishes in value, and there is no time for gaining enough new experience. See Figure 1.1.

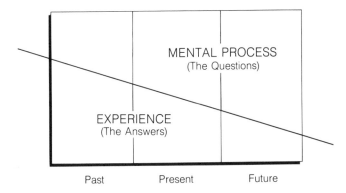

1.1 Experience and Change

The mental processes an able manager uses are conceptual. He operates on two levels at once: attending to the task and watching himself in action, how he is doing it. Thus he not only can watch, monitor and steer his thinking, but is able to learn from the experience. To assist this process, he constantly and consciously adopts processes which will enable his 'snowball' to gather extra skill exponentially. He is not trapped inside his objective analysis or his subjective feelings or his imagination, but is willing to draw on any of his different faculties according to the demands of the situation. He stops to think when he sees himself rushing on too blindly. He is free to do this because he is self-aware, and able to do so because he can recognize specific characteristics of his task in terms of specific characteristics of his mind. He has some kind of language for matching the two, whether or not he has ever heard of the work outlined in this book.

Conceptual skill is strategic. It enables the person who has it to know where he is in relation to a situation, to visualize the possibilities open to him and to choose the one to go for; or to recognize that something is not known or not right, and to work out the thinking that is needed. He can 'see' his thinking, watch it, listen to it, get the feel of it. It is this 'feel' for what is required that leads to his being in control of what he thinks and hence what he does. He is conceptualizing what the task ahead of him requires. Such an activity is of a high order and it has been posited that this separates Man from the animal kingdom. Can animals rise above the mere instinctive and think ahead too? Plainly there are levels of conceptual skill. If you can conceptualize only at the lower end, this limits effectiveness in the world. Those who can conceptualize at higher levels can offer a special kind of leadership.

Questioning Skills

The easiest way to spot conceptual managers is from their questioning. At one level, it's impossible to live in the world without busily conceptualizing all the time in tiny ways; on the same lines, most people are often asking questions. 'What's this for?' 'When will it be done?' 'How many are there?' 'Why are you doing this?' Some men and women have raised questioning to a high art. Questions are the driving forces of their thinking; they form the very structure of their knowledge. It is through their questioning they create meaning in the world. The conceptual manager seems to pluck questions out of nowhere. His questioning structures enable him to predict the kinds of information that will be useful in advance of any knowledge of the subject.

I have met some good questioners in my time, and at first it was to me uncanny how they could raise an issue so clearly, without any experience of it. My tutor at Exeter College, Oxford, Greig Barr, could do it but I put that down to his knowing much more than an undergraduate. This usually was the case with managers I worked under in my early days in commerce. Their questions were stimulated by their experience of having done the job I was then doing. In contrast at a slightly later stage in my career, I vividly recall the amazing way that Richard Lewis, then chairman of GKN Servowarm, used to enquire of things about which I knew a lot and which he knew very little indeed. During the war he had been in Intelligence. When I knew him he had founded several businesses in GKN of which he was also chairman, so he had a wide range to span. He was never burdened with paper, and yet commanded the central ground by the shrewdness of the questions he chose. One question might penetrate deep on a narrow front, and another might give me six weeks' work to bring a proper response. But all his questions seemed to be useful ones, and I learned a profound respect.

Looking back, I can see that his questioning first helped him identify useful information and second put the answers into patterns that made them useful. He got the maximum meaning from the minimum data, and his briefcase was ever slim. He was especially good at logical analysis of the situation, 'as is', but this is a quality of many able managers. On reflection now, for me what makes him a conceptual manager is that he would also invariably raise the issue of change. It was as if he had two axes in his mental map: one vertical for what could be derived from the 'as is' and the other horizontal for what might be explored with change in mind. A conceptual manager always has some form of comparator for his first line of thought. Lewis used one as a cross-reference for the other. I did not see it then, but he was asking questions that were cutting across current inferences and extrapolations, challenging assumptions, looking for the unexpected angle and for whatever might be surprisingly better (or worse). Although GKN was a business that began in 1769 as one of the founders of the Industrial Revolution, Lewis was far from being restricted by its tradition. He was at once both sound and questing. As my mother used to tell me, he 'used his head to save his legs'. He made a few questions go a long way. He was a conceptual manager.

The Origins of Conceptual Toolmaking

The tools introduced in the following chapters take many forms because while being essentially conceptual they have been deployed in a variety of ways to meet the practical needs of individual people. For me, a tool should be whatever its user needs it to do. I expect and encourage people to adapt my tools in whatever ways make them more of a help. That said, it is more efficient to find tools that can each do many jobs and for over 20 years I have devoted much effort to the search, design and development of anything that makes thinking easier or more effective. In case any passage in this book sounds elitist, I should say at once that my mission has been to enable people to over-perform, that is to perform better than might normally be expected in view of their intellectual horsepower. My professional education as a schoolmaster had led me to understand that there was a certain innate intelligence that was basically unalterable for each individual. The same might be said of physical capabilities such as an eye for the ball or explosive power or pole-vaulting agility. What appeals to me is to confound the predictions based on such limited factors so that people go beyond their apparent potential and individually out-perform those that are more naturally endowed. Ironically, it is often the most able people who are first to grasp hold of a tool and in using it they actually widen the distance between themselves and the less able. But at least they lead the way.

The Foundations

The body of know-how on improving mental performance that I have built up in my consultancy work is now comparatively extensive: it has certainly been hard-won. Foundations of a kind were laid when I was responsible for management education and development in Rank Xerox in the sixties. Developing other managers is the most effective way to learn for yourself. For a few years I went through intensive self-education, voraciously devouring all the management journals that came across my desk, personally attending many events outside the company, seeking out all the latest developments. In Rank Xerox we prided ourselves then on being ahead of the game, or at least trying to be. I discovered that mental tools gave a leading edge so it was during these Rank Xerox years that I started to make my own tools.

Subsequently I spent more than five years in Kepner Tregoe (KT) as managing director of their UK company. This was a wonderful accelerator of my own development, not only in managing an international business but also in learning how to teach the rational side of thinking. Many of those I was teaching were top level managers of some of the best companies in Europe, of higher calibre than myself of course. Yet it was possible to add value to them and their operations: the secret was not in me but in the tools I was deploying. KT methodology was well developed in its own sphere of interests and to high standards. And from Rank Xerox days onwards I had some tools of my own that I developed.

In 1975 I set up my consultancy with the mission to encourage more creativity in business. How on earth could this be accomplished? It was a daunting task but also a joyful challenge for me. I invested a whole year on my own R & D with the objective of building enough know-how in the shape of tools for the teaching of creativity to be able to deliver results for future client organizations. Amazingly some of those original tools are still in use today. I hope that does not mean that I have not done enough development over the past fourteen years! Development is really what drives my business as well as my philosophy. The need to improve the form and presentation of the conceptual tools has been an ongoing and continual source of my R & D effort ever since 1975.

The Philips Project

Strange to say this syndrome was important even to the joint development project with Philips (1977–81) that was to produce such a significant acceleration for conceptual toolmaking. The project is described in Chapter 3 and its outcomes inform most of this book. My point here is simply that the work we embarked upon seemed then so avant-garde as to need a great deal of justification even within Philips itself whose project it was. Actually the need to win support and acceptance internally may have had as much positive as negative value, for it made sure we were extremely cost-effective during the four years of the project, and also that we changed many things that were not acceptable enough to work.

The project was called DEVA, the shortening of a Dutch word for

Skilful Thinking. Here was a business organization, Philips of Eindhoven, enabling a small group of professionals within its manpower development function to undertake the sort of assignment that would normally belong to a university. Of course Philips has always been justly famous for its R & D investment, which even extends to pure science and pre-development in electronics and associated areas. But this was research into thinking skills, in an organization with thousands of good minds among its then 400,000 employees round the world. I felt really privileged to be the only external consultant in the team. I was invited to work with them because of my somewhat unusual combination of experience in management, rational problem-solving and creativity research.

It was more than two years (1979) before we put the results of our work into print. Until then, everything we produced was by photocopier. Yet the tools we had made were operational in several locations in Holland and we had developed on-site managers to teach others how to use them – we called these local managers 'mentors'. Our philosophy was to develop tools that worked when not in the hands of their originators. This meant as much field-testing and feedback as was necessary. Once something was printed it would be frozen, and its development inhibited even if change proved to be needed. I believe it was a good strategy. We did actually go for four-colour printing of the tools in 1979 and the eventual physical format of the conceptual tools proved to be important. I now think that the concentrated effort demanded by decisions to colour print have a real value in conceptual R & D. The freedom of experiment needs to alternate with the harsh finality of the large print run.

The other discipline I want to mention here is that of delivering results. Theory, as said earlier, ought to work. Our R & D process actually had to pay its way in the delivery of management development courses where participants expected to learn something that would add value to their part of the organization. Anyone who teaches managers knows that the 'learners' constitute a hard taskmaster. Although the intention is to help them achieve their objectives, course participants are a sort of market-place and although their wants are not always what they need, they must 'buy' what you bring to them for their learning to be successful. Tools they can't or won't use are no use. Thus the chief criterion for any part of our R & D output was that it helped managers get results. Some ideas didn't and they were dropped.

1981 brought the end of the DEVA research project as such but I have continued the development of its initial output ever since, both inside and outside Philips. All of my clients have benefited from the work and have also stimulated further development because of the needs I had had to meet in them. Now the challenge is to write it all into books, for a wider audience can be reached by broadcasting simultaneously than can ever be reached by a small consultancy like mine. The whole point of teaching thinking tools in the way I do is that they are interactive and alive. Reducing them to written book form is quite a challenge, especially if it is not to be too great a challenge for the reader! However, doing so should give a boost of a different kind to the ongoing development process.

Looking back on these fifteen years of work, it is hard to resist some feeling of achievement in having played a part in bringing some truly original research to fruition. I have not only done the research but also brought it into the world and applied it in many different practical management situations. Left to itself Philips would have simply let it go in the upheavel of massive reconstruction in 1981 when the research project came to an end. The two key people involved in the project inside the organization left, so I had to become the product champion from outside Philips. I felt the responsibility for this quite keenly. If you look around the market place today you will find that most of the thinking tools available stem from research work done many years ago. Not much that is really new surfaces and makes a significant contribution. Of course it is not an easy path to follow, bringing something entirely new to managers. They doubt before they even begin to grasp what is on offer. I have had to find ways to overcome the natural propensity of conservative managers to reject what they haven't already heard of, what hasn't already had the stamp of respectability placed on it. Another aspect to this was the limitation of my own resources. To build a base for continued development by taking the tools to new organizations and winning openings to work with managers, I had to concentrate on establishing a track record to demonstrate the real usefulness of the tools. Without far-sighted individuals in the organizations listed in the Acknow-ledgements, I doubt whether the work could have survived and grown as it has. Now it has reached the point where I am able to license others in these organizations to take the work on, and Philips is just embarking on their first licensing programme. My story is typical of those you would hear from any inventor – the long haul from discovery to implementation on a sizeable scale.

Managers often ask me in what way the conceptual tools I teach them are unique. Their uniqueness lies in the model of thinking on which they are based, which is described in Chapter 3. This is not a model grounded in neurology or brain waves, or left-right dominance but in totally fresh investigation into the way we use language to convey what we mean. By penetrating to 'intention' we discovered the patterns of will in the mind that cause people to think one way or another. Such patterns enabled us to build new tools which take into account the natural propensities people have to think idiosyncratically and to marry their individuality with the demands of any task they have to do. Thus they can better match their thinking to their work.

Because I often teach people how to access and integrate their creative faculties they sometimes ask me 'Is this like de Bono's work?' While de Bono's early work in the 1960s did impact my own development, I am bold enough to claim that the research we did in Philips took the understanding of creativity into a new dimension.

Treating any one kind of thinking, especially 'creative' thinking, as a god can be counter-productive. Conceptual managers will not fall into this trap. They manage their minds and the situations that confront them at a meta-level. Even when directing a particular kind of mental energy towards a situation with the special force it needs, they keep their balance. They sense when to redirect their mind as a different approach is needed. They are conceptually aware of the options at their command. It is this optimizing of the direction of mental energy which results in real creativeness. This is the conceptual manager at his best and it is to this situational awareness that I have made my special contribution.

For fifteen years it has been a mission for me to find ways to help managers release their creativity, and to make organizations more creative places to work in. Most of my work has always been to do with innovation in some way. I am a start-up man. I shall not attempt in this book to evoke the creative experience. Creativeness has an affinity with humour; utterly spoiled if you have to explain it. A special kind of publication is needed to give lively interactive stimulation so that the reader can learn by doing. What I shall attempt to show here is how the creative faculties must be included within all conceptual tools so that managers embrace the widest possible concept of relevance and beyond.

Conceptual Integration

What really matters is how to integrate relevance with creativity, where the conceptual manager excels. Relying on relevance alone is too limiting. Many people have felt it better to extend into the wider area of feelings. Much behavioural training has been sited solely here. But it is simply not good enough either, to confine oneself entirely within the subjective and the personal. Feelings must be related to what is sound and rational as well, otherwise bridges fall down, systems collapse and order is drowned in a sea of emotion.

For a few years I took the other route and made the mistake of focusing too much on the creative field. It was my way of compensating for the lack of creativity in the business world. My first conscious recognition of my own creativity came in the 1960s during a half-day on creativity in a management programme run by Rank Xerox in Noordwijk, Holland. The group was given the now famous exercise of individually listing as many uses of a paperclip as possible in a matter of minutes. To my surprise my list was miles longer than anyone else's. It was a revelation to me that I was at all fluent with ideas. From my childhood, growing up under the influence of my father who was a portrait painter and my mother who was a gifted musician, an elder sister and an older brother both with beautiful singing voices, another older brother who wrote poetry and composed, a grandmother who was a concert pianist and a grandfather who was an architect, I had taken it that I was not of their creative ilk.

Following the Noordwijk experience my interest was roused to explore further. Before he died, I started corresponding with Alex Osborn, the father of brainstorming, and joined his Creative Education Foundation, Buffalo, USA. Creativity became a hobby which was reinforced when, two years later, running a course myself, one of the managers remarked on my unusual and prolific use of analogy in the way I taught. Putting two and two together, all too fast, I twigged that I might be more creative than I had ever thought.

Today my emphasis is upon drawing the flow of ideation into the domain of relevance just as much as the other way round. I look back with some sadness that it took me so many years to discover and then release my own brand of creativity fully into my work. Not wanting others to suffer the same confinement I have made it a prime ambition to show managers how to bring creativity and relevance together directly into daily problem-solving.

My ideal of the conceptual manager is one who has integrated his thinking, and who is able to work consciously and congenially with all his mental faculties both in his job and with family and friends. The path towards integration never ends. It has been a long haul from those days of my first recognition of creativity to the present book. Nailing my colours to the mast, in more ways than one, this is a summation of half a life-time's work.

2

Conceptual Tools

Since time immemorial, Man has made tools. Primitive Man developed tools, devices and weapons of one kind or another for making survival less nasty, brutish and short. Over the centuries the relationship between his tools and his knowledge grew into what could be called his technology – a coherent process for dealing with physical matter, for farming, building, cooking, washing, entertainment, fighting, and so on. Using tools, you both create and control the conditions under which you operate in the world. Your life, for instance, in the jungle would be very different depending on whether or not you had a machete. Lose your paddle in a canoe and you would be hoping there is no white water ahead. Robinson Crusoe was fortunate indeed to salvage the ship's tool-chest from the wreck.

The essential function of a tool is that it gives its user an advantage. It either enables him to do something without which he could not do it at all, or it helps him do it better, faster, more easily and so on. Man has always been distinguished from lower animals by the enormous range and complexity of his tools. It is by their tools that you can recognize the level of development that different people have reached. In this book I make the metaphor stretch from the restricted sense of a physical implement in the hand to a mental tool for the mind and for thinking. With every year of progress, thinking takes over a larger share of life, not only in adding value but even in recognizing what value means.

As a child I grew up in a tiny cottage in Essex, England, by the River Crouch, in considerable poverty. My father was a portrait painter, an exceptionally gifted artist, whose work was hung 'on the line' at the Royal Academy when he was only 16. My mother was gifted too, a pianist and composer, the daughter of a concert pianist. Although we had little money, our home was a centre of attraction for many cultured and interesting people. At one time my father had been part of the community of artists at Ditchling which included Eric Gill, David Jones and Philip Hagreen.

In my father's studio, an old boathouse, I learned a reverence for tools. I watched him at work, holding my breath lest he should send me away for being a nuisance. He was notably a portrait painter but believed in exploring many forms of art from book illustration to religious abstracts, lettering to carving and even experimented with painting in colours that would be amenable to photography. He wasn't only a poet but a craftsman too having studied under the great Romney Greene to learn cabinet-making. A true Renaissance man, he worked in wood and metal and even made some of the tools with which he worked. When I was seventeen he built an eighteen-foot sloop virtually single-handed. His exquisite precision and skill with tools was an example to me. And so was the ingenuity with which he fabricated whatever was not available, for example, the steaming system for making planks bendable. He would readily agree, if he were alive to read this now, that his very paintbrushes were tools, just tools that by nature were endowed with a supreme flexibility.

Tools Add Quality and Extend Us

I am using the idea of tools as a metaphor to propose that people use mental processes as if they were tools in their minds. They manipulate them with their mental rather than their physical muscles. Sometimes they are conscious about it; more often, like me in my young adult life, not very conscious at all. As I explained in Chapter 1, I was in my thirties before I discovered that I was using a specific mental operation or tool to produce my wild ideas. (I now call this tool 'Symbolise', but this is to jump ahead.) Up till the moment of this discovery I thought it just happened by some personal quirk of fate.

The revelation that came a bit later was recognizing that metaphorically speaking there were in my head a whole series of different instruments for thinking. Each tool performed a different operation. As soon as I recognized one I could buff it up and make it even more useful. I came to see these tools as an extension of myself. The results I got with them depended to a large extent on how well I handled them. This meant not only knowing what I had in my mental kitbag, but also choosing to bring the right one out at the right moment. I also found that although these tools were inanimate, by my association with them consciously, they taught me. As my father loved the tools of his trade so I learned to love the tools of management – thinking tools. He would have been the first to point out to me that such tools were as much in the domain of the painter as of the manager, for the hand of the painter only executes what has been thought by its master.

What does a person hope for when he picks up a tool? It could add strength. A pulley or cog, or even a wedge, will direct a small amount of human force in such a way as to multiply its impact. Other kinds of tool add strength of a different kind, to grip harder with a spanner or pliers. A tool with conceptual rather than physical leverage is the Pareto principle. It is one of my favourites. It gives an instant grip on the few things that really matter. I can expect for instance that 80 per cent of my revenue will come from 20 per cent of my clients. Now that really does give me a lever for marketing.

Do you want perfect accuracy and precision? Then you might get hold of a pair of callipers or a micrometer. A management tool equivalent would be the checklist of questions for an investigation into the cause of downtime; always the same questions, regardless of the situation. This kind of checklist is a tool the professional trouble-shooter must have in his back pocket, if it is not engraved in his skull.

Some tools are good for ensuring completeness, like balancing scales which indicate when sufficiency is reached. Many accounting and inventory control routines do this. Reliability and consistency are often achieved more readily with a tool than through a person working freehand. Stencils make the repetition of an exact pattern or lettering possible even for someone quite unskilled. Templates ensure that a groove is cut to a constant depth, for example, in a piece of walnut for the dashboard of a Jaguar. Using them guarantees exactly the same shape and size time after time. However much people hate filling them in, standard forms are just such a tool for ensuring consistent information. Business cannot do without them. The demand on managers is to design formats that are conceptually sound both in the questions they raise and the layout provided, so that they actually do help people to think well. A poorly designed tool wastes time and energy and misses valuable information.

Some tasks require the use of senses beyond our natural limits.

Image-enhancing instruments such as telescopes and microscopes are used to manipulate, stretch and focus sight beyond the norm. Some situations are too complex for the mind to handle unaided. Managers then use devices for manipulating data: algorithmic flow charts, organization trees or wheels, or any of the graphic representations of numbers developed in statistical methodology. Other kinds of tools extend creative artistry and craftsmanship. Think of the subtle and beautiful creations from the paintbrush, the calligraphic pen, and the airbrush. Even here there are conceptual equivalents in the management and mathematical models that reflect subtle complexities in a simple, elegant form: from S-curves and Gauss-curves to catastrophe theory or the Moebius strip. Small wonder that these models can be seen as the expression of the highest form of art. Yet they are also creative and practical tools for the manager, giving insights into reality that cannot be reached without them.

There is barely a single human activity without a tool to grace it. And what do we do if we haven't got the tool we need? We adapt. We turn a screwdriver into a chisel, we use a knife as a spoon, we make scissors into screwdrivers, bamboo canes into fishing rods. We are all toolmakers. Managers do the same with their thinking tools, though it is to be hoped that when they cut corners or make too much of a temporary jury-rig, they are at least aware of it, and alert to managing any consequences.

What are Conceptual Tools?

Physical tools provide familiar examples with which to examine conceptual tools. Should such examples be necessary? Long experience has taught me that conceptual tools are not apparent to managers. They are concealed in the head and for most of the time invisible. We can see something physical being used, but in the normal business environment we do not actually observe conceptual tools since they mostly function hidden within the mind. A connecting bridge from concrete physical tools to abstract conceptual ones is needed. All tools help you to perform better, to do a better job. Physical tools help you do things better while conceptual tools help you to think better. The funny thing is, thinking is not yet recognized by everyone as itself a form of doing.

Conceptual tools are made by thinking for thinking. They include models and maps, frameworks, thinking routines and checklists, codes and symbols, conventions, procedures and systems. Figure 2.1 shows a collection of tools sorted into three levels, from the highly abstract general laws, like those of physics, logic and grammar, to data-specific checklists, like a recipe for a cake. As you proceed through the book you will meet the tools in this list, some of which you will not have come across before as they have not previously been published for the general management reader.

From the tools listed in Figure 2.1 let me draw your attention to just a few important characteristics.

The tools must be memorable because they will often have to be used straight from memory. For ease of committing them to memory they must have a physical format that is economical, vivid and simple as well as being sound. Probably my own poor memory has highlighted this for me. Perhaps because of the heritage from my father I always pay a lot of attention to the way tools are designed. They must look good, attract the eye and grab the imagination. As this book is purposely not a how-to cookbook we cannot show more than a few examples, and nor can we show them in colour. You can imagine the difference that makes.

Many of the tools in Figure 2.1 are universally useful and so they need to be in handy and portable form so as to be at one's mental fingertips. For the Philips project, described in Chapter 3, we had them printed on pocket-sized cards to make up a kind of conceptual Filofax. I have always found it useful to carry reduced-sized checklists and models in my diary. Now one of our associates in Germany is 'filing' them in his pocket computer. Of course the most portable device available is memory and constant usage gradually gets the tools into the natural bloodstream. Even so, I am not alone in finding physical cues and props of value.

The final point is probably the most important of all. All these tools are questioning tools. Either implicitly or explicitly they pose questions, in order to attract the kinds of information that will help to solve a problem. The art of managing is the art of asking questions from a sound conceptual base.

Most of the well-recognized management techniques come from the realm of number. Few of them demand high levels of mathematics, and when they do, it seems to make sense to let the specialists or professionals do the fancy work. It will be the job of people like those in Operations Research to explain what matters to

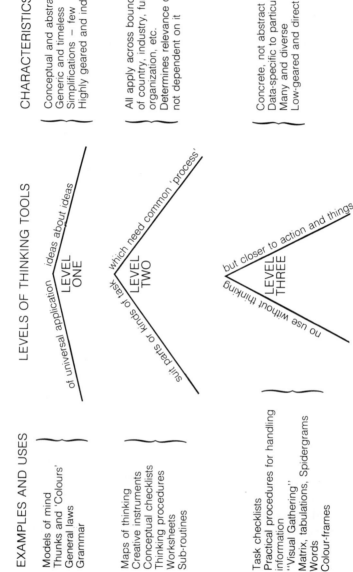

CHARACTERISTICS

Conceptual and abstract
Generic and timeless
Simplifications – few
Highly geared and indirect

All apply across boundaries
of country, industry, function,
organization, etc.
Determines relevance of data,
not dependent on it

Concrete, not abstract
Data-specific to particular tasks
Many and diverse
Low-geared and direct

LEVELS OF THINKING TOOLS

of universal application   ideas about ideas

LEVEL ONE

which need common 'process'

LEVEL TWO

suit parts or kinds of task

but closer to action and things

LEVEL THREE

no use without thinking

EXAMPLES AND USES

Models of mind
Thunks and 'Colours'
General laws
Grammar

Maps of thinking
Creative instruments
Conceptual checklists
Thinking procedures
Worksheets
Sub-routines

Task checklists
Practical procedures for handling
information
"Visual Gathering"
Matrix, tabulations, Spidergrams
Words
Colour-frames

2.1 Levels of Thinking Tools

the line executive in terms he can appreciate and work with. (I just hope that the story of the American President who needed to be told how to convert 2/7 into a percentage is totally apocryphal.) The tools used by the main line manager have mostly been fairly simple and straightforward methods for quantifying what is known or predicted, for revealing the shape and trend of events, for making relevant comparisons, and of course for analysis and synthesis of various kinds.

Who can manage at level three of Figure 2.1 without graphs, histograms and scattergrams; without pie charts and percentages and Venn diagrams; without the blessed matrix or decision trees; and perhaps above all without cluster analysis and system modelling? Increasingly, powerful tools like these are spilling out of the specialist areas into the mainstream of management's thinking technology. As a result, managers are much more able to deal with those issues demanding quantification, so that their judgements are soundly based. This book is not the place to go into quantitative techniques, except to acknowledge their power and value. They are extremely useful for representing complex reality in simple form so as to give insights from various angles. But quantifying models do not solve a problem for you. So I am concerned here with the wider conceptual frame in which they fit, and the thinking which determines when and how to call upon them.

The tools I shall delve into in this book were made from language. The enormous range, flexibility and capacity for growth of language has made Man into the conceptual toolmaker *par excellence*. Language is the best tool we have for identifying and naming something, so that it can be recognized again. At a high abstract level language includes signals, symbols and representations of all kinds. So images and pictures are a language, and so are music and dance, mime and gesture, architecture and higher mathematics. All human activities tend to organize themselves into their own special languages of images and words.

Words themselves are a special kind of imaging, of the greatest practical use in exploring and developing how Man thinks. A Gaussian curve of imaging would show at one end of the scale primeval picturing, and at the far extreme the most sophisticated and advanced abstract art, but in the massive central ground would be words. Words are the majority of your images. Imaging is crucial to thought and therefore also for tools for thinking with.

There are many ways to represent the kinds of thinking required for a particular part of a task. As an example, Figures 2.2 and 2.3 show the two faces of an instrument which can be seen as a means of putting structure into brainstorming and challenging an existing set of constructs. Figure 2.2 is full of specific questions and Figure 2.3 relies mostly on its visual layout. Together they make a tool which through the pattern of its questioning recognizes how something is at first perceived, from different clusters or viewpoints. By purposefully changing one's position, new and often original and creative ideas can be brought forth. It is not appropriate to go into the workings of this instrument here. The point that I hope makes itself is that when it comes to memorizing and therefore accessing tools under pressure, the visual tool (Figure 2.3) wins hands down. On the other hand, if you have to get down to specifics, you will certainly benefit from those questions in Figure 2.2.

In the work I have been doing over the past 20 years, I have discovered that managers and knowledge workers do not realize how significant the words are that they use in forming the tools of their thinking. In my view, while the learning and use of quantitative tools should never be overlooked, training needs to pay much more attention to language, since quantitative models and hard numerical data must ultimately fit into the 'soft' frameworks of meaning and values. The nub of conceptual tool using and toolmaking is the language you use, and thus how you put ideas into words. Words are usually easier and quicker to make than pictures, a sort of shorthand syndrome in reverse. Best of all, we can speak them.

This means that we can, as it were, send any message by radio or telephone to someone we cannot see, yet the receiving person has the facility for converting the sounds, delivered by a sequential linear signal, into a parallel spatial image or pattern of images. It is as if the listener can actually receive by fax. So to follow the analogy, you can decide when to send a picture-fax for conversion into words, and when to send words for conversion into pictures. In practice, the choice is often determined by the kind of person at each end, whether his own human fax is better at sending or receiving. This means that when creating tools for other people I have to take into account whether they prefer pictures or words. In practice I combine the two.

So words are pictures in another form, often more simple and condensed. Of course the converse of this is true, where it can take pages to say what is in a picture, a logo, a cartoon. But the creation of the right picture to convey your idea might well be so demanding that you turn to words. Words are more readily portable, the essential currency of information. They are the most useful tools known to us. They have the extraordinary characteristics of being flexible and rigid at the same time. What engineer wouldn't be delighted to make a physical tool with these characteristics. My tools rely therefore on both words and pictures.

Much of Man's thinking and its development has been facilitated by putting words together in strings that occur frequently. As with computer programs, strings are portable sub-assemblies that save mental work. Aren't we all taught strings like 'who, what, where, why, when and how'. I don't know about you, but I can often complete the sentences of someone talking to me without listening to his every word. I rely on strings of meaning which I can recognize without actually decoding each word and sentence in full. By not having to focus on his every single thought, I free my mind for what is difficult within what is being said. This string technique pops up all over the place in my tools. I call such strings 'subroutines'. They enable me to build new maps from sub-assemblies very quickly, in the sure knowledge that these ready-made components are soundly constructed and won't let me down.

We all form patterns out of everything, and thus are better able to handle many complex things at once. The ways we connect and separate meanings of words, the richness of our vocabulary, the range of our associations, all shape our ideas. Very able people do all this more purposefully than the rest, because they use their patterns as tools. Every proverb for instance is a pattern and a tool. 'A stitch in time saves nine.' 'Too many cooks spoil the broth.' 'A rolling stone . .' and so on.

All my tools are built out of patterns that I have recognized by observing myself and other people when they operate effectively and ineffectively. The conceptual thinker sees patterns in the millions of phenomena that are just noise to others. If he is a toolmaker as well he can represent what he sees with models. Models short-cut the need to re-invent the wheel each time. They condense what would take many pages of words to explain into a dynamic and integrated image which embodies the essence (or pattern) of many similar experiences. Figure 2.4 is an example of a model for planning. It represents the learning gained from many experiences of making plans. You can use it repeatedly to help you with your planning if you can spot the occasions when it is relevant. Of course, beware that your concept of

PROBLEM/element ....

ATTRIBUTES: WHAT IS IT MADE OF?

What are its features and characteristics?

What reference points & boundaries categorize it?

On what plane or continuum is it? With what others?

STRUCTURE: HOW DOES IT HANG TOGETHER?

What elements and forces combine to give the thing its structure and balance?

What is the variety, mix, proportions between them?

What relationships work the system, within/outside?

What is its context?

What if we distorted in space, time, extent, force or direction?

PURPOSE: WHAT IS IT FOR?

What must it be or do to be what it is?

What criteria show its quality?

What needs/dependencies do they reflect?

Who owns or belongs to what?

FUNCTION: WHAT DOES IT ACTUALLY DO?

What benefits occur as spin-offs?

Are there consequences unforeseen?

Are there better substitutes/alternatives?

What else could it do? Further uses?

Synergy?

MEANING: WHAT ELSE COULD IT MEAN?

How else could it be analysed or described?

Simulated? Any analogy useful?

What if we used a different medium, language or discipline?

Is there a deeper truth underlying the explicit?

What is just not visible, or understood?

Should we see a new thing, or seek something new in it?

2.2 Pattern of Description – specific questions

Pattern of Description

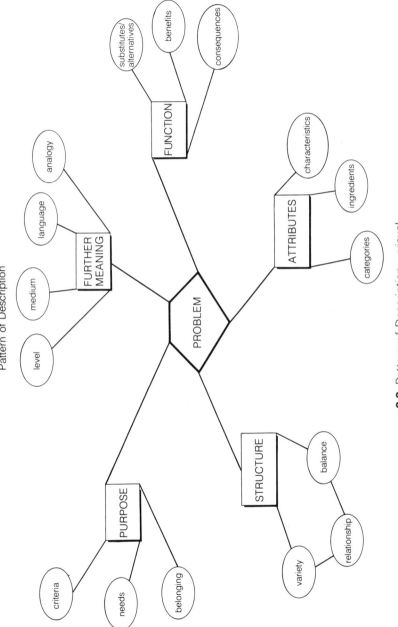

2.3 Pattern of Description – visual

relevance isn't too tightly drawn. It is all too easy to suffer from premature hardening of the categories.

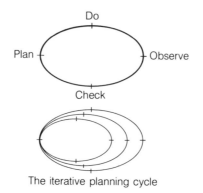

The iterative planning cycle

2.4 Adapted from Deming's Model of Planning

Forming patterns and making models is the essentially efficient way of problem-solving, especially in handling and even looking for information. It is my thesis that the capacity to do this modelling is the heart of toolmaking. When a manager can make and use visual models, using language and layout to show the significance and repeatability of the pattern he has found, then he is operating at the highest conceptual level. He is creating the means by which he can capitalize on his experience more productively for himself, his staff and his customers. Let me explain this a bit more.

Thinking can be seen as asking oneself questions and providing their answers. Questions turn out to be one of the major tools in a person's thinking repertoire. The very questions that drive thinking reflect patterns pre-formed in the mind. These patterns are in fact models, but most people are unconscious about them. They do not realize their thinking is bound in by them. The models they build for themselves, or that they have imbibed from others, actually operate as a circus ring around which their thinking habitually passes. If the models a manager carries in his head are unconscious, he will not have access to the patterns that drive his questions. We will be trapped into routines of thinking over which he has limited control. Everyone possesses the innate skill of modelling or making patterns. The purpose of my work has been to awaken in people a curiosity and thirst to grapple with their own pattern-making capacities, so that they turn what is an unconscious and poorly exercised inheritance into a conscious and highly effective skill. Once they can manipulate the models in their minds, to create and recreate them anew, they will connect their thoughts better. They can, in short, understand, predict, plan, map and observe their own thinking operations.

Connecting is a vital aspect of thinking. It makes experience portable from one situation to another by identifying what is suitable to generalize. Learning French should help one to learn Spanish and even to learn Dutch and German, though it might not feel like it at first. Most of the vocabulary is different, only some more abstract principles are shared and they might not at first be obvious. The art of spotting connections, overlaps and similarities between apparently different experiences represents a key learning skill. Good learners turn every experience into a pattern to store for future reference.

To use any tool at all requires this connecting function and without it every single event in life is so unique as to demand total attention as if being faced for the first time. The result of this would of course mean no learning and no progress.

Sometimes I find it difficult to persuade people that their thinking processes can be mirrored in some useful tools. Many top-class operators retain a feeling that their own area of specialism has some mystique that puts it beyond any form of analysis, and therefore unyielding to any kind of tool. They feel they have an art, or a knack, or something supremely qualitative about their work which resists conceptualizing. Surely, some work does defy analysis far longer than other kinds. It may be hard to observe or record what is really happening, or hard to interpret, to find the key patterns.

If these special few who excel cannot themselves pass on how they do it, does this mean their experience is worthless to anyone else? Have they made no improvements to their own approach since they began, which they could name and describe? Will their successors have to start from scratch? Are they unable to offer any advice or share their wisdom or reproduce the knack in any form at all? Can they not even tell us what not to do, what is not a good way? Surely they can recognize an imposter when they see one? If all the answers are 'No', then we have no tools yet for their arena.

The problem faced by businesses today is not that they don't know they must learn. They know it all right. What they really want to learn is how to do the learning better. Attitudes like those of the specialists above do not help. My many years of work with scientists, who like to think their methods of work are beyond understanding, have demonstrated to me that it is possible to penetrate into even the most esoteric skills. I try to give an insight into this in Chapter 8. Not that I do the penetration. I provide the conceptual tools so that they can model their own processes and describe them to one another in the common language explained in Chapter 3. The benefits to the business, when scientists can improve on their methods, both individually and more especially in team work, is calculable in millions. It is a recommendation to everyone to improve his ability to model his own thinking processes.

Awareness of Tools

An essential element in my work has been to invite managers to examine their own tools. When running a programme to develop the thinking of a group or a team, I will ask them to write down the main elements in their process of coming to a decision. Among the thousands who have responded, there are wide differences, largely because the elements are fashioned to suit their own temperaments and thinking styles. Very few have ever asked themselves how they reach decisions or discussed it with colleagues in spite of the fact that managers are supposedly paid to make decisions. They all have ways of doing it but, if challenged, are seldom able to defend their method with any confidence. They just do it.

What has become abundantly evident is that managers are fuzzy about their own tools. They muddle their conceptual levels. A typical defensive position will be 'I operate situationally, so I am always changing the way I think'. However when you observe the way that person really works, dealing with various problems, his belief is all too seldom substantiated. What usually turns out, in practice, is that he is data-driven in his analysis of how he thinks and that he is judging his process by the differences in the data he is handling. The data differences obscure his view of his own processes. So of course every problem appears situationally different.

What I then try to do is to get him to penetrate to the underlying processes which drive the way he thinks about the data. Persistence reveals that there are always process elements strung together, process strings, which he repeatedly uses. These are his personal conceptual tools. The elements vary from person to person. The language to describe the elements is varied too, even in the same organization or department. A dominant personality, though, who coaches his staff, will transfer his tools to others and thus develop a pool of people who have a set of common tools. But this is rarely encountered.

Another significant finding has been that while managers talk linearly they think spatially. Their personal tools can be drawn onto paper in spatial configurations because their grasp of their own conceptual tools is usually diagrammatic. In real-time activities they access their own thinking tools in holistic swoops to inform the linear steps of discussion in meetings or for writing reports and letters. This means that managers readily pick up on the visual tools I have made because they dovetail with their own natural thinking processes.

There seems to be some difference between what I will call deskwork, which is more likely to be reflective and written down, and real-time thinking, which is usually done with others or on the hoof. Investigations I have made have shown that people are much more conscious about the tools they use in what I am calling deskwork situations than real-time. Take the strategic continua listing shown in Figure 2.5. Managers I come across are much more likely to pull such a list out of their desk drawer if they are alone rather than in a meeting. Somehow business cultures haven't developed in ways that make it possible for people to refer to pieces of paper when they are with others, unless the paper carries information on it. Figure 2.5 carries nothing that could really be called information. All that it offers are a set of general polarities to help clarify one's position in any situation. In reality there are several positions along any continuum. The effective person makes himself aware of where he is standing when establishing objectives for a particular decision. He can then test whether his stance is really appropriate for the situation. Where along each continuum is it best to position oneself now, so as to achieve the most useful balance? And how will this balance affect one's judgement? By the way, with a list like this, switching one's position on a hypothetical basis does wonders for new strategic insights.

The same tools, of course, can be used both real-time and for deskwork thinking. To get them used real-time, methods of displaying them for all to see are necessary. Over the past twenty-five years the flipchart has made a significant impact on the speed and quality of meetings. It is used for making thoughts visible as you go along. It might seem laborious at first sight, yet it raises effectiveness

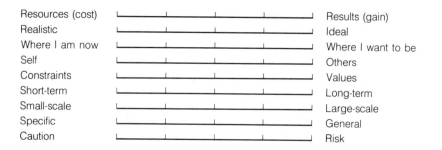

Resources (cost)		Results (gain)
Realistic		Ideal
Where I am now		Where I want to be
Self		Others
Constraints		Values
Short-term		Long-term
Small-scale		Large-scale
Specific		General
Caution		Risk

2.5 Strategic Continua for Setting Objectives

significantly. Now the new methodology of Visual Gathering (VG) which I have introduced into many companies, has made a further quantum leap in the gathering and handling of ideas, values and information, making the flipchart feel out of date. The VG process displays the thinking steps which will be followed, usually in the form of trigger questions. Everyone can generate and share their thoughts simultaneously using chits, which can be moved around, sorted and re-sorted. The thoughts that are stimulated are collected and organized using tools of all kinds to orchestrate everyone's efforts and shape them towards the results sought.

If this sounds a recipe for chaos, it should be said that disciplined freedom is not a contradiction in terms but an ideal state. The freedom is necessary in order to produce and allow the best efforts of everyone concerned in the Visual Gathering. The discipline is provided by the skilful use of conceptual tools by whoever is in charge. If he can come with good questions for inviting useful information, and good procedures for bringing it all together, then he draws out high quality thinking in everyone concerned. He has actually combined the best aspects of deskwork and real-time thinking with tools.

Our education systems have neglected to teach us to be conscious of how we think. As far as I know there is no systematic use of inventories in schools to help children identify their personalities and thinking styles. Perhaps it is thought to be too early in their stages of maturation to let children look at their learning styles in any measurable way. Of course, a good teacher has a very useful idea of the learning styles of those in his or her charge. I have been encouraged by letters and phone calls from teachers, who on reading my first book have seen the applications of my approach to thinking for schools. I am being asked to produce a thinking styles inventory specially for secondary-age children. Such a request has come from India where they are already experimenting with methods for teaching conceptual skills.

When managers meet together, what often happens is that the unconscious but natural thinking style of the most dominant personality will hold sway and push the information into some kind of useful shape for him and maybe for the others. What is needed to make the most of working together simultaneously is a process that is common to all. A group needs tools in common to recognize and deal with the diverse or unfamiliar information each member brings separately to the meeting. Between them people try to manage their meetings with processes as diverse as the information they bring. Unless a corporation actively trains its personnel to use the same thinking tools, quite fundamental management tasks are carried out in a wide variety of ways. Because the tools they are using are hidden in their heads, usually subconsciously too, people are unable to make clear to each other what they are using. Their different processes cause conflict, disrupt their relationship, and certainly diminish their effective output.

The question to be asked then is, 'If you are totally unaware of your own processes, is it proper to call them tools?' I believe not. They must be somehow separate and you must have some consciousness of their effect. Yet there is a paradox. When you use a tool with perfect skill, it becomes so much a part of you that you are hardly aware of it at all. This is as true of great sportspeople with their racquets, clubs and bats, as it is with consummate managers and their thinking-tools. Perhaps this explains how it is that you can be a great performer without knowing why or how you do it, and that you can learn to do something so well that you cannot recognize you are putting into practice something your company has taught you. The implications for the learning organization of this paradox carry very far indeed. A tool without a label can easily get lost. It is my thesis that we have to label the good tools, using a common language, so that people can recognize them. Such a language was born of the DEVA project which will be explained in the next chapter.

Generic Tools

Every handyman has a number of tools that are hardly ever used because they are, like a mitre, specific to one particular job. He also has a few that can do almost everything. Who would be without a knife? How could civilization have grown without a pen of some kind? Whether it is a concrete tool, or abstract like numbers or an alphabet, the more central it is, the more diverse the applications for it, and the more use it gets. Tools that perform very fundamental functions, such as a blade or a wheel, are central, generalizable to many thousands of tasks and called generic. Of all tools these add the highest value. They are the most worthwhile to learn about. There is certainty of return. Because they will be used often, the skill in using them will grow exponentially. There are, of course, degrees of generalizability. Today we are amazed at the versatility of the anvil when there is a blacksmith who really speaks to it. Yes, that is the phrase he uses. In the early days of motor cars, he could make almost anything needed for their repair. Ultimately though, the generalizability of the anvil is fixed by its physical limits. Thinking has no limits. It informs and determines everything you do, thus occupying the most central ground. Thinking tools are generic, although there are degrees or levels as shown in Figure 2.1.

Figure 2.1 is an attempt to simplify the tools to be discussed in this book on just three levels of abstraction. The highest level, ideas about ideas, includes models of mind and general laws, and is almost akin to philosophy in its universal and timeless nature. Such tools come from having distilled many complexities into simple form, so they are few in number. They are like the hub of a wheel in being so highly geared and indirect that they might not impact a particular situation without the person applying considerable intelligence and imagination to connect the general to the specific. If he is successful, these tools will produce big results. They apply to a very wide range of situations indeed. When such a fundamental activity as decision-making is modelled, it reveals the essential characteristics and operations involved and will inform all and every single choice you ever make about anything. I will not be covering this model here since I included it in my first book, *The Colours of your Mind* (Fontana, 1989). I shall, however, look at a model of learning later. If businesses model learning properly, it will make a difference every time they wish to take advantage of experience, whatever that experience might be. Such highly abstract and simple conceptual models are for practical purposes eternal.

By contrast, when it comes to the tools at the lowest level in Figure 2.1, you need lots of them in many different shapes and sizes in order to cover all your diverse specific tasks. New ones are being invented all the time, and are often actually made *ad hoc* for each new situation. They are directly practical and so close to the job that a checklist on this level will usually include content as well as pure process. A checklist of criteria for a new invention could include factors standard for that industry such as serviceability; or the more general criterion of disposability which perhaps ought to apply to every product ever made; or the even more general criterion of reversibility, that is, whether the effects of the product/process can be undone. Whether such criteria are applied each time or not, and whether they are treated as absolute or comparative, the checklist has done its job as a tool if it has at least raised the issue and made you take a decision about it. The practical implications are obvious when we think for instance of nuclear fuel. These kinds of tools, especially if data-specific, have a narrow field of vision compared with high-abstract models. Yet they are closer to solid things and to action, and so their usefulness is directly obvious.

In the middle are a range of process tools which suit whole classes of similar activities and apply across all boundaries of industry, organization or discipline. While these tools often take on physical form, they are essentially conceptual, and more generalist than narrowly professional. You can join a multi-disciplinary working party whose members use expertise quite unknown to you, and yet you could all enjoy the same process for dealing with certain aspects of the project you are all managing. The creative instruments shown in Figures 2.2 and 2.3 are good examples. People can work well with these operational tools even without a clear understanding of the more fundamental models they are relating to. A group can work in a meaningful way to anticipate threats and to reduce the risk entailed, without necessarily holding the same holistic map of planning or decision-making in their heads. Every tool has its range and its boundaries, and it is possible to work within them effectively although a system-wide common language of tools is an advantage.

Multi-disciplinary tools are the tools for our time. They are the tools people need if they are to think together, for team-work and collaboration. In practice, all fields of human endeavour have their own tools for operating, and these represent a large part of their corpus of expertise. In finance, concepts such as ratios, fixed and variable costs, capital v. revenue expenditure, balance sheet presentation, are basic necessities for thinking about the business. Engineering, production, distribution, sales and personnel each has its own body of concepts. Increasingly now process-concepts that start out in one field are being recognized as portable to others. Engineering control systems are used in finance, economics, personnel and development. With some adaptation, many processes are multidisciplinary. They have become formulae that are generic.

Modern corporations require advanced tools for thinking across all professions and disciplines, although few businesses have actually realized it yet. Why is this, I wonder? Ordinary education is supposed to provide the necessary raft of transferable skills upon which to build a life's experience, beyond the three Rs of reading, 'riting and 'rithmetic. In England, the old grammar schools were actually based on the universality of grammar as a model for thinking. To read for a classics degree is still seen as the best all-round course of study to equip the higher echelons of this society. Science and mathematics are valued in the USA as necessary disciplines but too tough for many people and too narrow for them to act as generalist bridges across all realms of thought.

When young people enter a profession they learn specialized and advanced conceptual tools, but not how to make them generic. Each profession and discipline has its own conceptual tool-kit. Professional hubris restricts the extent to which these useful tools are disseminated throughout society. I was interested to learn recently that Lorenz's early models of the functioning of the nervous system had no feedback loops. Cybernetics had not reached the ethologists. Useful specialist tools would have much wider application if they were spread through other disciplines. Obvious examples are found in systems analysts' work, organization and methods, and finance, but all functions use techniques others could adopt.

Transferring tools across boundaries becomes much easier to do when the generic elements of which they are built are recognizable and made visible and user-friendly for everyone. In the work I've been doing with business organizations over the past fifteen years, some truly generic components in all tools have been recognized from which everyone can even build new tools as they need them. My work with Philips uncovered a family of concepts which reflect what I believe to be fundamental components of thought. If so, they are the tools to make tools. I introduce these in the chapter that follows.

3

Tools to Design Tools

Out of an alphabet, you can make any words you need by combining letters in different ways. A few notes are enough for all the music in the world. Using his palette, the painter can produce any colour he wants and there is no end to the variety of pictures he can make. The table of elements accounts for all known physical matter, and ten numerals for the universe of number. By analogy, is it possible that a small number of mental operations could be responsible for all the thinking anyone ever does? In this chapter I describe the discovery of just 25, illustrate them and explain how they are used as tools to design tools.

The building blocks of alphabets and numbering systems look something like this:

$$\text{Letters} \rightarrow \text{words} \rightarrow \text{sentences} \rightarrow \text{art}$$
$$\text{Numerals} \rightarrow \text{numbers} \rightarrow \text{formulae} \rightarrow \text{science}$$

A few letters or numerals become millions of different words or numbers. From these millions are constructed, through grammatical and mathematical rules, all sentences and formulae which in turn become holistic art and science. The few at the far left grow into the many which in turn make a whole of high level complexity within. Following a similar sequence, a gradation of conceptual tools could look like this:

$$\text{Mental operations} \rightarrow \text{instruments/ subroutines} \rightarrow \text{maps/ models} \rightarrow \text{thought}$$

There are, of course, many alphabets and numbering systems and it is important to recognize that none is perfect for every human need. George Bernard Shaw spent his energy in vain trying to get improvements to the established English alphabet. However, because they work and because they are adopted and used by many peoples, the alphabets and numbers in use throughout the world provide tools which make effective communication possible. The system of tools in this chapter needs to be viewed in the same light.

The Search for a New System of Tools

In the 1970s, investigation in Philips, the multinational business based in The Netherlands, revealed that individuals and departments drew upon a wide range of conceptual tools, and every manager in the course of his life had adopted, adapted and made his own mix. No-one knew whether his own set of tools was sufficient to do his job well enough, nor how to identify what was missing and what might be needed to improve performance. There was only a strong feeling that the standards of problem-solving in the widest sense of the word should and could be higher than they were already, and that existing methodologies were not good enough to deal with the issue. In 1977 a far-sighted project was initiated to address these issues. I was invited to join a small project team as its external consultant. Our goal was to come up with a generic methodology for dealing with business problems of all kinds – in other words to create a comprehensive tool-kit which would give Philips' managers a competitive edge conceptually. The project was conceived and developed in the Mental Skills section of the department concerned with the design of world-wide management development programmes.

Our approach was to start afresh, deliberately 'forgetting' all we knew about the conceptual tools already in use in the business world. We pursued a semantic path, hypothesizing that the richness and variety of the thousands of words and phrases in use disguise a few, we didn't know how few, fundamental thinking patterns which create and shape the flux and flow of thoughts. We knew of Chomsky's work, of course. In the sixties he had discovered the patterns that structure all language. In contrast, we were setting out to look for the patterns behind all conceptual thinking. Our idea was that if we found the natural deep structure that shapes everyone's real-time thinking we could construct from it a conceptual tool-kit for managers. It could be used to improve their existing thinking tools and most especially those tools used in real-time where we saw the greatest need to be.

Although we were operating in a corporate context, rather than confining ourselves to business jargon we embraced vocabularies from all walks of life. We did this because we guessed that the deep structures of thinking would be present in all kinds of discourse: navigational, trading, artistic, athletic, electronic, educational, financial, social and so on. As we were genuinely aiming eventually to create multi-disciplinary tools, we had to include all disciplines as our sources. Our research process began by collecting thousands of phrases and word groupings which we clustered and re-clustered to identify the similarities and differences between them at succeeding levels of simplicity. We did a lot of work to extract the essential meanings that lay within all that variety and richness. We classified into hundreds of groupings, and tried all sorts of relationships between them. The essential questions we posed as we tried to recognize the pattern in each successive grouping was 'What is common between these words and phrases?', 'What would I be trying to say if I used these words/phrases?' and 'What result would I be aiming for?'. We were looking for the intentionality in people's minds when they use words. This concept of intentionality was fundamental to our whole understanding of thought. We saw all thought as purposeful, even when it was being purposefully purposeless. Of course this idea is the subject of moral philosophy and religious doctrine, but we saw it as a means of getting at whatever goes on in the mind when a difficult issue is handled.

Here is a glimpse of some word groupings we struggled with, giving nonsense names to help identification:

ZU
Let's get down to specifics
Small fleas on bigger fleas' backs
The immediate cause is . . .
The ultimate effect is . . .
Tell me in a word . . .
Helicopter/microscope

MORF
Try this twist
Imagine that . . .
Re-organize

Conceivably . . .
To push it to extremes . . .
Draw it on a balloon
By skewing this . . .
$+ - \times \div$

SO
Break it into bite-sized chunks
This is part of something bigger
Where does it belong?
A new way of grouping them would be . . .
What do these have in common?
Now suppose they are not the same
Why can't we combine this?

So each classification we came up with had a dual purpose both to be a practical tool and to encapsulate a fundamental pattern of intentional energy in the mind. As we discovered what seemed to be meaningful and useful clusters, we gave them nonsense names so as to easily identify them. For example SO, a tool for joining and separating ideas, and ZU, an operation of sliding between levels like a zoom lens. SO was an early version of what is now 'Distinguish' and ZU of 'Set Level'. As the work progressed there were several families of these nonsense names which we found a useful device as thought-buckets.

To check how useful our embryonic mental operations were likely to be we tested them continually with several levels of managers at the sharp end, to keep the development of these mental tools in line with managers' real needs. Their practical down-to-earth reactions to what we delivered were a necessary counterbalance to any intellectual overelaboration.

We had our own criteria for tool design against which we measured our work. The following represent the main ones:

- The resulting tool-kit should possess simplicity, clarity and integrity.
- It should be inviting and appealing to experienced and junior managers alike.
- The tools in it must be easy for managers to learn.
- They should make a recognizable difference to a manager's effectiveness on the job.
- They should be quick and effective for managers to use real-time on the job.

- The tools in the kit should not number more than x because managers cannot be expected to use more than a handful at a time.
- The tools must be generic, so that they could be used by absolutely everyone in absolutely every situation where quality thinking was needed, yet they must be specific enough to be useful in depth.

  Ideally, they should be so fundamental that they could be used as tools to make tools, wherever the need arose.

By rigorous testing and re-clustering over two years we honed the number of mental operations to 50, which we estimated as too many for anyone to be able to handle as a generic tool-kit. At one time we boiled them down to seven, and quickly found these were too densely compressed to be useful. At the outset we had aimed for 23 for its elegance as a prime number and because it appealed to our sense of humour; but the clusters eventually worked through to 25, functioning on several levels. We had a rule that reality should never be sacrified to elegance, so 25 became the final number. We were bold enough to believe we had codified in these 25 the roots of thinking, the basic mental operations that shape all thought and, in the boldest leap of all, that they could be used as tools to design ever more tools to meet whatever problem life could throw up.

Introducing the New Concept

As soon as you introduce a new concept, you have to identify it with a name so that it can be recognized by everyone wishing to refer to it. To be fully useful you must be able to say it aloud as well as write it down. Naming a new concept has its problems: what root language to choose; what sound to convey meaning; what associations to invoke? Although in English most of our vocabulary about thinking seems to have its roots in Latin or Greek, this is an accident of history, and generally I favour Anglo-Saxon simplicity and Icelandic strength. As a project team based in Eindhoven, The Netherlands, we were actually working in both Dutch and English. We learned a lot by translating from one language to the other and back again: it is never the same! It was important to invent a new word to distinguish the concept from 'thoughts'. So I coined a one syllable word *Thunk*. The 'unk' sound is to convey an earthy energy surging from the deep, because Thunks precede thought, as the intentions behind or underneath what you think. Moreover this energy symbolizes another aspect of reality, namely that the range of thinking represented by the Thunks is by no means limited to the drily cerebral and analytical precision that most people see as intelligence. What they embrace includes the influence of the body on the mind, as well as its reciprocal; it includes the subjective motive forces and feelings; and it includes the influence of the spirit and the imagination. So the emotional warmth and energy of the sound runs against the rustling of dry parchment associated with some intellectual disciplines. The other flavour of the 'unk' sound is of course humorous. Some people have reacted very sharply against the name, perhaps because they see an incongruity or dissonance between the cerebral nature of the concept and its sound. Thought is no joking matter.

Naturally, the name chosen was intended to be associated also with 'think'. Thunks are mental operations, mental activities, the thinking intentions which actually produce and drive all thinking and action, whether consciously recognized or not. Thunks are not themselves thoughts, but rather they give birth to them. They are the processes that vitalize and move your thinking to produce the data of thought. They represent all the things we are doing with our brains that produce thoughts. An early insight that came to our project team was that thinking was better represented as verbs than nouns, a tremendously alive and active phenomenon.

In the collective name Thunk, those of us in the project team saw ourselves as expressing a new concept in the philosophy of knowledge (*scientia*). This needs a bit of explaining, and analogy might help. When you throw a ball, your intention is to throw . . . an intentional action. You can see the throw taking place, and you can feel it when you do it yourself. You judge the distance, aim, and then throw, hoping the ball reaches its target. Even as the ball leaves your hand, you probably know whether it will reach or not. Physically you can perform a number of basic intentional actions with the body like throw, catch, run, jump, and so on. Out of the basic actions you can create any number of complicated and beautiful dance routines, gymnastic feats, sporting extravaganzas. Likewise, each Thunk is a basic intentional action of the mind. Out of the array of 25 Thunks you can make any number of complicated and elegant thinking-moves as I shall show in subsequent chapters. I do not want to labour the point here, but this special nature of Thunks is the secret of their value as conceptual design tools and their unique place in the philosophy of science. At this point my aim is to describe the Thunks in order to provide the basis from which to explain the design of other tools with them. You may wish to skim read this section and then use it for reference later when reading the chapters on maps and making them.

The complete family of Thunks is arrayed in Figure 3.1. The hexagon presents a sort of analogue model of your mind in a holistic display without bias as to the relative importance of its six main divisions. Other visual layouts are used to show differing relationships between the various Thunks, according to whatever is most relevant for the purpose. For example, the colour-frame, which comes later in this chapter, is a layout intended for handy problem analysis. This array in Figure 3.1 relates all thinking to the requirement to take action. The three Super-Thunks, Judge, Describe and Realise, group around the one in the centre, which represents the verb 'to do'. By its positioning, Do symbolizes the belief the Philips team held dear,

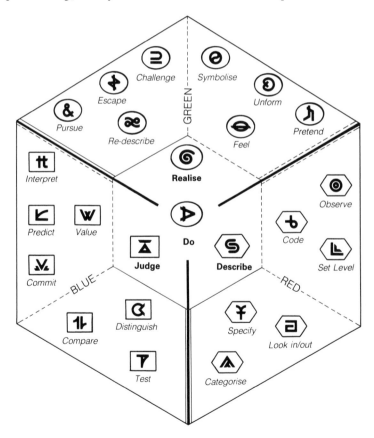

3.1 Thunks: a vocabulary for thinking

that all thinking is pulled together by the need to do something better than it would have been done without thought. For us, thinking was supremely purposeful. Upon its quality rested everything you valued, what results or outcomes you deserved to achieve, how well your actions actually matched your intentions.

In this hexagon model you see displayed the complete tool-kit of your mental operations potentially ready to serve whatever task you have to do. In later chapters I shall look at how you select which tools to use when, from the array. When you activate any one of these operations in your mind you purposefully engage your mental energy towards the output that particular Thunk is designed to achieve. If I may resurrect the physical muscles analogy once more: the deltoid muscles lift the arm, because it is their function to do that, so that, for example, you can take a book from a high shelf. Similarly, the mental muscle Specify focuses your attention to detailed accuracy, say to check the figures in your company's balance sheet. The function of Specify is to cause your mind to attend for example where a particular source of income or expenditure appears in the accounts.

In the sections that follow I shall describe the function of each of the Thunks so you get a brief but rounded picture of the mental power they represent. I actually have several thousand papers which cover the Thunks in all their many forms and a special manual, *The Book of Thunks*, soon to be re-published. In writing this book I have had to weigh where to place the emphasis, and I decided that rather than extended portrayal of the Thunks, a brief overview at this stage would be most helpful in order to lead into the crux of this book, the mapping tools.

Interpreting the Hexagon
The Central Thunks

While 'to do' is the central drive of thinking, the three Super-Thunks clustering around it deliver judgement, or information or ideas. Judge, Describe and Realise are on a higher or more central level than the rest, so they each encompass all the Thunks of their own domain. The goal of Describe is to establish what is known to be true, what is or was. The goal of Realise is to find something new, that is, beyond what is already known to be true, what might be. The goal of Judge is to conclude what is right, what should be. These three goals draw the mind's energy in three different and often conflicting directions as the different tenses of the verb 'to be' indicate. All thinking emerges from these three directions of the mind. Every time a person thinks, he is actually selecting a direction for his mind, however unaware of it he may be. Like the four main points of the compass, these three super-tools help you to choose in what way to look with your mind, that is literally to direct your thinking.

In this array of the alphabet of thinking, there are several codes. The most obvious is the name of each Thunk. Our Philips project team gave each of the Thunks a friendly, homely, familiar-sounding name whenever we could. While it seemed a sound idea to create for the collective name a brand new word 'Thunk', we decided people would not want to confront the jargon issue with every one of the 25. Much care was taken to select each name so that it expressed the nugget of meaning it represents. Each Thunk is a verb, a short action concept, to indicate the activeness of 'doing' thinking. Yet there is a wealth of substance within each Thunk. To distinguish the names from their common usage in writing, I use a capital for the initial letter. When speaking I say, for example, 'the Thunk Predict, the Thunk Feel' and so on. This need to distinguish led to the second code, the symbols shown in Figure 3.1. These symbols are not just for fun but of vital practical importance. In Philips we had the vision that we were creating a language which could cross national and language frontiers. So with international road signs in mind, we designed symbols that could represent every thinking intention (Thunk) in any language. Each pictogram does attempt to reflect the essential purpose and meaning of its Thunk, and yet all have been created so that they can be written with two or three quick strokes of the pen. They serve as a shorthand, even when using one's own language.

Another code is the shape *around* the Thunks symbols. Those Thunks that contribute to the Realising of new ideas each have an elliptical field, those that support the Description of truth have a hexagonal field, and those that effect Judgement have a rectangular field. Corresponding to the three Super-Thunks and also to the shape of their respective fields, the three main Thunks groupings were given a colour-code. Colours were chosen for the visual impact they bring as well as a simple, easily recognizable and memorable code. People can remember the three colours and what they stand for quickly. And for building conceptual tools they have the special bonus of adding meaning without having to add words. In terms of visual layout, then, the colours are invaluable for tool-making. The colour code itself is metaphorical, bearing no relation at all to real colour. Blue, red and green were chosen because between them they create all the colours you see on your television screen, and just as between them they create white light, so they symbolize the wholeness we were attempting to achieve with the model of mind. These three colours are also most readily available in felt pens and biros, so any manager can get hold of them without special dispensation from the purchasing department! When it came to writing this book, my intention had been to by-pass the colours altogether, since they have been explained and illustrated in some depth in my first book *The Colours of your Mind* (Fontana, 1989). However I found it such a handicap to do without them that they will be used here after all.

The colour code is interchangeable with the Super-Thunks, since blue stands for Judge and so on. When it comes to the hard and soft aspects of the colours, which embrace subgroups of Thunks, this is the only way of distinguishing them in speech. So when I speak of 'hard blue Thunks' I am referring only to Test, Compare and Distinguish; by 'soft green Thunks' I mean Unform, Feel, Pretend and Symbolise. This is a useful classification, because each of these subgroupings work together in ways that I shall explain below. In the hexagon the solid lines denote hard colours and dotted soft. This hard-soft code will be given more substance as I come on to describing the hard and soft Thunks.

Just one more point about the colour code. In practice, and in spite of some obvious disadvantages of the associations that people carry with colours, like the 'Green' movement, or party political colours, they serve a very useful purpose. They help people clarify what they mean when they use words that are in regular use at work but which are beset with a multitude of interpretations. Take, for example, judgement. The linking of the colour blue to judgement causes one to say 'Why on earth? After all, I know what judgement is.' Unfortunately, every individual has his own ideas about it. There is no real consensus. By looking afresh at the sense of judgement through the colour code, 'what should be', it causes everyone to sharpen and focus their definitions and brings conceptual clarity. This can be repeated with every Thunk word, and with any other word one cares to offer. Thus it encourages people to examine their understanding of words in everyday use and how they use them to do their thinking. The colour code, which is outside normal business language, provides a new common language from which better thinking can flow. I made the point about common language in the first chapter and I shall come back to this theme again.

The Hard Thunks

When teaching I often refer to these Thunks as 'hard thinking tools'. Hard is not meant in its literal sense and neither does it mean difficult. It is a metaphor for describing a characteristic which these Thunks all have in common. As tools they deal with the more tangible side of thinking. They help you, the user, to be more objective than subjective with your thinking. They require you to think explicitly and quantitatively about a problem rather than implicitly and qualitatively. In general they lead you to define your thinking clearly and somewhat absolutely. They help you put boundaries around constructs, place information in watertight categories, make use of solid realities even if it is to violate them, and apply absolute logic. Between them, these three groups of hard Thunks provide the means for constructing all the tools needed for objective operation. Thus they are used to build not only the concrete structures through which we organize all life in the world, but also the concrete structures of the inner world of our own minds. If we took the design of the human body as analogous, we could speak of the hard Thunks as more like bones than muscles.

Hard Blue

When a task needs logic to see it successfully through, then the Thunks to use will be found in the hard area of Judgement. You will Compare certain facts against others; Distinguish the pattern that may be hidden within those facts; Test the soundness of the conclusion you will have drawn from the pattern.

Hard Red

A task needing facts requires Thunks from the hard area of Information. You will Specify the information required, using very accurate and systematic questioning that covers every angle. You will secure the most complete account possible, by Looking Inside the matter and Outside it with equal energy, even turning the whole thing inside out in your diligent search. And you will Categorise all findings in the most orderly and efficient way, so that full and proper use can be made of them by your judgement when the time comes.

Hard Green

If the task needs a new approach, to go beyond the obvious information or conclusions likely to be used by everyone (else), then the easiest Thunks to use might be in the hard area of Ideas. You will Challenge the hidden assumptions in your mind that would otherwise constrain your freedom. You will Escape from the merely rational, finding the fun in seeking the hidden paradox which will justify sailing into the wind. You will muster all the ingenuity you have so as to Re-describe what you can see in as many ways as possible so as to violate your natural perceptions. And you will Pursue and persist with the new lines of thought you are developing, continuing to look for something else beyond your first thoughts, relying on the number and variety of your attempts to achieve a few really good solutions.

Thinking about a problem is done to improve your chances of getting wherever you want to go. You must come out of automatic pilot and start consciously thinking. The hard Thunks may often be the first we grab hold of consciously, because they have more of a tangible feel to them, and seem to be very explicit in their association with the thinking that goes on above the surface, on the table, objectively upfront. There are many books published about thinking where these hard mental operations occupy almost the entire ground. There is a directness about operations that require no-nonsense absoluteness, specific accuracy of description, firmness, consistency and reliability. This is why some people loved mathematics at school because at least until you go to more advanced levels of beauty in the field, you can actually get all the sums right and score 100 per cent. Logic seems to work and is easily defendable. Even the green Thunks, when they are hard, work because they are making explicit and tangible challenges to existing information and judgements. They are using what exists or is known, and purposefully violating the current interpretations of the facts, to offer the chance of a new resourcefulness about them. The person who exploits his perceptions with lateral strategems is so obviously making a direct assault, that it is easy even for the most hard-headed and rational person to appreciate what he is doing.

The Soft Thunks

I have separated the description of the soft Thunks from the hard to emphasize the qualitative difference between them. Choosing between the Super-Thunks is the first level of selection that a conceptual manager has to make when problem-solving: 'Do I need to tackle this from a blue, red or green angle first? Which is most appropriate with these people now? Should I be encouraging them to be having ideas (green) or do we need to close down and come to judgement (blue) because of time pressures?' The next choice is whether to move to a hard or soft aspect: 'when do I go into hard or soft blue, red, green to sort this out? I've got to get the details first (hard red), or have I? Maybe I can hold on that and establish a clearer sense of our criteria (soft blue). Two of the team are pushing to widen our perspectives (soft green) so maybe I should start there.' With such vivid images from the colours he can make use of Thunk tools while 'on the hoof'.

Judge		Describe		Realise	
Hard Blue	*Soft Blue*	*Hard Red*	*Soft Red*	*Hard Green*	*Soft Green*
Distinguish	Value	Specify	Observe	Re-describe	Feel
Compare	Interpret	Categorise	Code	Challenge	Unform
Test	Predict	Look in/out	Set Level	Escape	Pretend
	Commit			Pursue	Symbolise

Soft Blue

When a task requires a person to give full scope to his subjective, personal feelings, then the Thunks to use will be found in the soft area of judgement. What you Value will ultimately rule your thinking. You will Interpret the situation surrounding you as if your perceptions were more than bare, unconnected pieces of reality. You will be willing to go beyond the indications and extrapolations of the facts when you Predict what you believe will happen. And you will Commit to a decision with the finality that ensures action.

Soft Red

If the task needs you to draw on your experience to gain a fuller picture of truth, then you will find the Thunks for this in the soft area of Describe. You will tune in and amplify all your senses so as to

Observe whatever is there. You will select and use the most appropriate Code or instrument or medium with which to receive or convey the information needed. And you will Set the Level of enquiry or communication so that reality will not be lost from being out of focus or on the wrong scale.

Soft Green

When the task needs new realms of imagination, you will pick the Thunks in the soft area of Realise. This really means letting the universe into your mind, as distinct from the 'hard' approach of going out and changing what you know. Yet, like listening and welcoming and being alert, it is not passive but active on a subtle level. You are deliberate when you Unform your mind, consciously causing the categories to soften their iron boundaries, and allowing your constructs to become as malleable as wet clay or copper wire. You will Pretend that something might be so, playing roles and creating hypotheses and scenarios of (im)possible futures, entirely without commitment. You will lay yourself wide open to all the conceivable associations between the ideas in your head when you Symbolise. And allow yourself to listen in to the weakest signals of intuition, that is what you are able to Feel, even when there is no apparent evidence.

Discussion

It should be clear by now that the metaphors of hard and soft are far from meaning difficult and easy. In practice, it is possible to see that the reverse could almost be justified: that the hard operations are more easy than the soft. So any association of the latter with the slang 'soft option' is right off the mark. Another suggestion often advanced by managers on first encounter is that the hard Thunks relate more to the computer while the soft ones are for the human being. After all, the early and most obvious tasks for the computer involved number-crunching, lists, categories (Specify and Categorise), and of course logic (Distinguish, Compare, Test). The first attempts to use computers for generating ideas have been in morphology, where they are endlessly patient in generating multitudes of permutations (Re-describe, Pursue). Computers are not so good at the soft operations, even the 5th generation that is so keenly awaited. They are beginning to be able to choose how to present information so that it is user-friendly (Code). They do not have their own values (Value), but they can Interpret to a limited extent whatever values they are given to work with. As far.as I know, the computer's ability to have an intuition (Feel) is non-existent. And the computer is not yet known to smile.

It may be helpful to suggest other characteristics distinguishing hard from soft thinking. Your hard-headedness likes analysis, structure and organization. It is happier when information is evident and countable. It operates more with obvious and explicit relevance that can be justified by some fairly rigid formula and may even use a tangible mental device or instrument in order to explore for new ideas. It likes things to be literally rather than metaphorically above-board, and provable in the outside world. By contrast, the soft side of your mind operates from a more inner strength, as it were from deep below the surface. This part of you goes on feelings and impressions that are often elusive, even when exerting a strong influence. It can even reject plain logic and specific quantification as being tiresomely irrelevant because they might conceal a deeper level of reality. The 'soft' mind is by nature more open to inspiration and vision because the hard walls that can be built around one's categories will be treated as if they were permeable membranes. In short the soft model of thinking is more like biology than mechanics.

Nonetheless, it is too tempting in so short an introduction to jump to conclusions that would be merely simplistic. It is not fair to reduce the role of hard thinking to the second part only of the man/machine interface. There is value in recognizing that as human beings we need the machine within our ghost, as well as vice versa. Our body would be as useless without the hard rigidity of its bone structure as without the soft strength of its muscles. We need our hardness to be efficient, our softness to be effective, with our mind. Everyone knows thinking has to be holistic; on the other hand, it is useful to divide up its functions so as to recognize, control and liberate each of them better.

Far more important is to see the intention of this model of mind to be truly all-embracing. 'Thinking' is taken to mean all and everything that goes on within a person's whole being, in order to reach a conclusion about what action to take or not. Many models relegate thinking to a narrow sector of the whole, like the way that we used to define intelligence and try to capture its measurement with IQ tests. Other models picture many levels of the person, from behaviour driven by instincts to emotional, cerebral, and upwards to the spiritual level. For their purposes, all these models have their own validity. In the Philips project, when we finally derived the colour model out of the Thunks, our purpose was not driven so much by philosophy as by a pragmatic search for a cognitive system for problem-solving in business. Yes, our approach was supposed to be a cognitive rather than an affective one: the implications in the affective area have followed afterwards as the inevitable consequence of pursuing the wholeness of thinking in the way we did.

When our efforts at codification arrived at the 25 Thunks, we had no plan to divide them up in the way they have eventually formed themselves. It was simply that even 25 was too large a number to handle easily in our heads, and by working with them in practice over a period we found they seemed to cluster behind the three leaders, Judge, Describe and Realise. It was actually a further two years before it emerged that each of these Super-Thunks had two aspects, and that these had enough in common to characterize them with the terms hard and soft. Then we found that there was a considerable advantage in placing all the domains of mind on the same plane, rather than on higher and lower levels. This reflected the even-handed choice that is available to anyone in using his mind: no one colour is better than any other and all are needed for total effectiveness: hence the image of the three colours together creating white light. We could then hold that our model was not normative but descriptive; it was not intentionally biased but dispassionate. A person could use it to hold up a mirror to the inner workings of his mind.

In attempting such an introduction to the Thunks, I am aware that you have not had any examples to make them alive in your experience. I had to choose between the value of such interruptions and the need to cover all the Thunks of the model in a reasonably short space. We may also run the risk of condensing the description with such economy that the hexagon model appears simplistic. As this book unfolds I hope you will come to appreciate the value of capturing in one single model so much conceptualization. It is the best I can do to reach a kind of user-friendly simplicity in cold print. All we know is that those who have learned about the Thunks live, in practice find the model a meaningful and useful reference. Although we have run through all 25 Thunks at breathless pace, I hope there is evidence in this chapter of the world of thinking that lies within each one. My purpose in the last few pages has just been to introduce them. I hope to show them in action in the chapters that follow; that is to show their divers functions as conceptual and practical tools.

Why 25 Thunks?

If our project had been undertaken in an environment of academic purity, it could have taken many more years of course, and indeed would probably not even have been started. We had a practical purpose in view, and that goal always drove us onwards to accept approximations wherever they seemed to work. Ideally, perhaps, there would be exactly the same degree of differentiation between all of the 25 Thunks, but this was not achieved. We always knew that there could be many ways of cutting up the cake, and in fact we came up with several versions, all of which are valid for different purposes. As it is now, each of the Thunks has special relationships with certain of the others. For example, within the hard blue sector, Test, Compare and Distinguish are particularly close as a working team to achieve sound logic. They also have especially close ties with Specify and Categorise (hard red). Distinguish works closely with Re-describe (hard green). These examples could be replicated in the soft Thunks as well. Code (soft red) works closely with Interpret (soft blue). In contrast there are greater distances between other combinations of Thunks. Unform (soft green) is not a happy bedmate with, for instance, Test (hard blue), nor Value (soft blue) with Escape (hard green). This reflects not only reality but our design purpose. We wanted to show the inner conflicts of mental operations, the struggle within the mind to co-ordinate its different thinking capacities. Of course this also applies between people, and we later developed a way of profiling these differences. Such profiling has become one of the most useful management tools to come out of this project. It is mentioned in Chapter 8, Conceptual Learning.

In seeking to identify a manageable number of basic mental operations, we had recourse to a number of condensing devices. For example, each Thunk contains both positive and negative, as if the polarities of 'Yes' and 'No' within the Thunk are at the opposite ends of the same continuum. This is comparable to saying that tall and short are the same thing, namely height. For instance, using the Thunk Specify, when perhaps negotiating an agreement, you can decide whether it is appropriate to use it to handle information extremely specifically (positive pole) or extremely vaguely (negative pole). The user of the Thunk is in charge.

A couple of sentences above I refer to 'using a Thunk'. You will find this phrase, or one like it 'using a colour', frequently in the way I write about these tools. I make it sound as if you can pick up a Thunk and actually wield it like a physical tool. That is exactly my intention and that is exactly the aim the project team had in mind, so that managers could metaphorically pick up the appropriate mental tool and wield it consciously to achieve a specific purpose that would help the task they were trying to achieve. A good craftsman picks the appropriate tool for the job. So also does a good craftsman of thinking. It is quite a step of the imagination to grasp this and then actually do it. Most of the time most managers are unaware of what mental tool they are using. That unawareness just won't do in a world that is racing towards intelligent machines and the global information society.

A further condensing economy is to use each Thunk either in sender or receiver mode. The analogy comes from radio communications. So when Realising ideas, one can seek, explore or invite ideas as a sender; and one can find, recognize or allow ideas as a receiver. Along the same lines, to Describe information can mean to ask for, tell or imply it as a sender; and to receive, know or understand as a receiver. When it comes to judgement you can influence a situation, prove something or persuade someone in sender mode; and at the receiving end, you can be influenced, come to judgement, and conclude or (dis)agree.

By far the greatest economy however was achieved by determining the level of thinking operation that would provide enough discrimination to be accurate, and yet be broad or rich enough to be practical. The human mind is probably the most complex system that exists: whatever number of thinking operations were involved in any model of it, each one would be incredibly rich in its depth and diversity. Yet to come up with a million thinking operations, or even a thousand, would be deeply unhelpful. The only solution we could reach was to settle on 25, as I have already described, and to recognize layers or levels in each Thunk which could always be pursued for a particular situation or purpose. Each Thunk can be turned into different kinds of tool for different situations. The anatomy of each one would be an inherent part of its description, and would also serve to show how it worked and how to use it. In working out the structure of each

Thunk, new tools were born. They were published for use in Philips in 1979. Two examples of these early Thunks tools are shown in Figure 3.2. Since then many forms of tools have taken shape, created by people for their own uses in many different organizations.

Tools for Tasks

In describing the research into the functions of the Thunks so far, I cannot emphasize strongly enough that the main purpose of all our efforts was to come up with a practical system or methodology for handling difficult situations of concern to managers. Right at the outset of the project, our focus was on the tasks managers have to do. Just as described earlier in the linguistics search, in looking at the tasks of managers we again abandoned for a while all the known models of problem-solving to be found in the management literature or actually in use in organizations. We meant to work from the grass roots up. But before long we had a rough taxonomy at a general level of problem types that seemed to apply to management work of all kinds at every level of an organization. They were:

> Situation Awareness
> What's Facing Me
> Develop a Plan
> Explain a Variance
> Making a Decision
> Gathering Information
> Set the Task
> Working with Someone Else's Plan
> Seek Alternatives
> Set Priority

We thus had something to concentrate on fairly soon. In this basic list of ten types of problem-solving task, there was nothing very surprising, and at that level it roughly confirmed work already done around the world (including that of Kepner Tregoe). Yet with hindsight there was at least one significant omission, namely the task of learning. Because this is now everywhere being recognized as a key management task, whereas then it was seen as peripheral or specialist, I have been working on the mapping of the learning process over the past six years and hope that I have now come to something useful, which is to be found in the chapter on learning (Chapter 8).

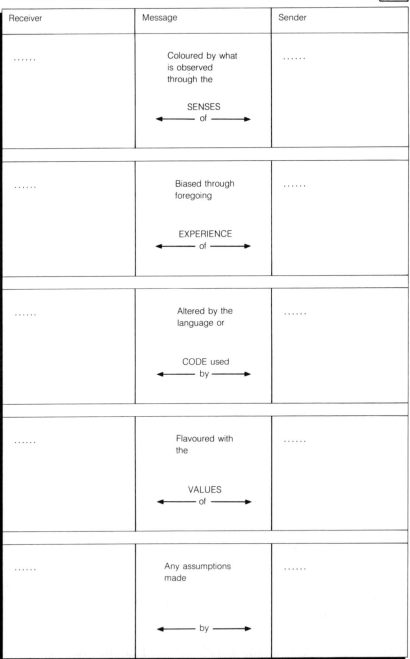

Receiver	Message	Sender
. . . . . .	Coloured by what is observed through the SENSES ◄—— of ——►	. . . . . .
. . . . . .	Biased through foregoing EXPERIENCE ◄—— of ——►	. . . . . .
. . . . . .	Altered by the language or CODE used ◄—— by ——►	. . . . . .
. . . . . .	Flavoured with the VALUES ◄—— of ——►	. . . . . .
. . . . . .	Any assumptions made ◄—— by ——►	. . . . . .

3.2 Two Thunks Tools

Present classification is . . . . . .

Separated are . . . . . .

We want to re-group because. . . . . .

What needs to be grouped together?

What seems similar but does not belong?

Distinctions characterizing these. . . . . .

TEST: Do these distinctions suit our Purpose ?

Labels for the new groupings. . . . . .

If you go to a high enough level of abstraction everyone with enough capability, experience and know-how can be brought to a sort of consensus or common ground on basic problem types. The real contribution of the Philips project team was the mapping of mind and task in the same terms, and the creation of a common language for both. These two faces of work, people and task, are different but so closely related in practice that the understanding of one fed into the development of the other. It is a dual model that we ended up with, of task and person. Since the majority of managers have no common language for recognizing either the task or what mental resources they possess to bring to bear on it, the tool-kit of Thunks was a breakthrough of breathtaking potential.

The Common Language for Person and Task

For the task we developed a connected system of tools of many kinds based on Thunks, all to do with how to understand the process of thinking required to get effective results. Sometimes this entailed making significant improvements on the routines of well-established methodologies. Always it meant designing tools on various levels using the Thunks model to build and quality-assure them in order to make information-handling more efficient and more effective. We were even led into developing a special kind of thinking process which we call a map and which will be explored in the following chapters. And we found a way to enable people to develop tools of their own.

For the person, we had of course the same Thunks model. The point not yet made is that those Thunks were by no means developed simply out of a linguistic analysis. In unravelling the nature of problems, what is their structure, what are the conditions essential for solution, what are the elements and components and how must they be related together, it forced us to keep switching between the anatomy of task and the anatomy of mind. What has the person got to deal with the tasks that he creates and confronts? What are its requirements and what mental resources does he have? When we had made a little headway in finding some embryonic thought-constructs, we could try them out by using them on developing our problem-solving approaches. A task is dealt with successfully because the process used works. In finding what are the key elements of each process, we could develop our understanding not only of the task-process but also of the mind-faculties used: they grew hand in glove.

I am in the business of thinking for business, not for the beauty of theoretical elegance and perfection. It is this pragmatic approach to their development that perhaps accounts for the robustness of a range of 25 mental operations that might otherwise seem no more than some theoretical speculation. As a set, they have been in operation now for a dozen years, the changes they have undergone being more a matter of development than of any significant correction. It is reasonable to expect that someone could come up with a better set and that we have missed some altogether. Indeed, I like to challenge colleagues and clients to find gaps, to pose problems that might tax the Thunks. One thoughtful dinner party host several years ago asked me, 'Where is "beauty" in your system? You don't have a Thunk for it.' As I see it the recognition of beauty usually comes through the use of the Thunks Observe, Code, Compare, Value and often Symbolise too. When you aim to create something of beauty, these are the Thunks you must pick up and use to give you half a chance of achieving it. Another kind of beauty is that found for instance in Mathematics. Here you could need a different run of Thunks, including Distinguish, Interpret, Categorise and Symbolise. By the Thunks you use you determine what kind of beauty you are seeking. Runs of Thunks will supply you with a focus on what is really meant by any concept in use. As I said earlier, there is much confusion about what is meant by terms in common management use. So far, having asked managers on hundreds of occasions to put forward activities to see if Thunks fail to interpret them, no one has been able to come up with any thinking he needed to do which is not covered by some combination of these 25. The model simply works.

Applying Thunks

Since the Thunks are a universal language, applicable to all situations that require thinking beyond what is instinctive or automatic, the applications are infinite. Any good merchandising of a product will tell you its features and benefits. I have spent the best part of this chapter giving the features of Thunks. Now for the benefits, which are to be found in all and everything. You can use the Thunks in all management activities to improve what is done, and in all walks of life. I would be very interested if anyone could discover an area of activity where they do not apply. In response to my first book, where I only described the colour level of the Thunks model, I have received letters of appreciation from a nun, a policeman, a science teacher, several systems analysts and computer experts, to mention just a few, plus many from consultants from all over the world who recognize that in their know-how business this model is dynamite. The rest of this book is devoted to showing the benefits of using the Thunks tool-kit for management work, and by way of introduction I shall conclude this chapter by pulling out two key uses which have benefited managers. The first brings benefits for people themselves, and the second helps people to handle tasks better.

Profiling People's Thinking Styles

The first application is in using the Thunks for profiling and developing people. I take it that the reader of this kind of book does not have to be persuaded that growth and development of individuals throughout their working lives is beneficial both for the individual and his organization. The significant benefit of this profiling is that not only does it provide the means for understanding and improving people's own thinking skills but also gives them a new language for thinking in. This combination raises the effective intelligence of an individual or of a group. They can generate and communicate a wider variety of ideas faster. They can ensure higher quality of information. They can make judgements more wisely, from the standpoint of sound logic and on the strength of personal integrity.

When I profile managers it is usually during a learning event using the Thinking Intentions Profile (TIP), which is a profiling question-naire I developed after the Philips research project ended. It is now available under licence world-wide. Organizations that want the benefits of spreading a common language among their staff can take up the licence for themselves. In the information sectors of the economy, where knowledge workers are the backbone of the business, it has been seen as particularly beneficial. The pay-off from raising the level of effective intelligence of the key people in an organization by just one per cent can be measured in millions.

Colour-framing Tasks

The second application is an instrument which directly helps to improve the ways managers match themselves with their distinctive thinking styles to their work. I designed what is now known as the 'colour-frame' a few years ago. Shown below, it is a way to describe either a person or the task he faces based on the TIP profiling format so that the colour-frame can be directly connected to the profile in the person's memory if required. Shown here are Thunks displayed in the colour-frame, to establish the underlying template.

Distinguish	Specify	Challenge
Compare	Categorise	Re-describe
Test	Look-in/out	Escape
		Pursue
——————Judge———————	—Describe——	—Realise———
Value	Observe	Feel
Interpret	Code	Symbolise
Predict	Set Level	Unform
Commit		Pretend

The hard Thunks are uppermost, the soft below. The frame provides 6 boxes which represent the appropriate Thunks in hard blue, soft blue, hard red, and so on. For example, bottom right represents soft green, Feel, Symbolise, Unform, Pretend. This 'digital' arrangement is more practical and easy to write in than the hexagon 'analogue'. The colour-frame offers a consistent structure of ultimate simplicity to remind you of all the mental operations you have at your disposal for the task. With three strokes of the pen you create the 6 boxes and the shape is ideally practical for writing into. You can take an A4 sheet or the back of an envelope or cheque book according to the emergency, speed or detail required. In a blank colour-frame, the boxes become data-bins or thought collectors, in which to record events or activities, preferences, or opinions, in short, live expressions in each particular colour. Anyone can remember what the boxes stand for in terms of hard and soft colours, or even the Thunks they stand for when that depth of detail is more useful. But it is most often used at colour level, hence its name.

How is it used? When working with managers we find that they like to use the colour-code for its vivid simplicity. So the colour-frame is a ready-made tool for them to take strides in their thinking when they need to sort out the elements that they have to deal with. You can use the frame to map out a job, to plan a speech or a report and to check someone else's. You can rough out your argument for a crucial telephone conversation, or a staff briefing. Each segment of the frame invites you to ask yourself 'What is needed here for this task?' Then you can set your thinking at the colour level or, when it is warranted, drop to the greater detail of the Thunks.

Here is a quick example of how a research scientist started to classify his work. Archiving fits naturally into the hard red box, and so would 'I love keeping accurate records of my research'. Both are examples of the Thunk Categories. The driving mental energy of an activity has been ascribed to a particular box in the frame.

Modelling an experiment	Archiving	Challenge accepted wisdom
——Blue ——————	—— Red————	— Green ——
Stop a project	Explain idea to Commercial Dept	Create hypothesis

The colour-frame can be used to describe either people or tasks in several ways. A situation can be assessed either in terms of relative importance or in terms of time sequence, say when you want to plan how you will tackle a tricky meeting.

Importance				Time Sequence		
4	5	3		5	2	6
1	2	6		3	1	4

The frame can be used to contrast what should be with whatever is the actual. A practical use is to contrast a person's view of the importance of an activity with the time actually spent on it. Given the frames below, the person concerned had better do something about his personal management of time, unless the importance does not determine how long he should spend.

Should/importance   Actual

1	2	3
4	6	5

6	5	4
2	3	1

It is particularly useful to compare and contrast the profile of a task or job with the profile of the person facing it. The model of Thunks and their colours is after all the first and only language which enables someone to describe the person and the task in identical terms. Imagine someone like Margaret Thatcher, the Prime Minister of Great Britain at the time of writing, attempting to design a more wonderful building than the Taj Mahal. I hazard my guess at her profile here. I am placing her thinking attributes in order of their significance as she seems to display them in public. For the design process I am assessing the faculties of mind in order of necessity to accomplish the task successfully.

Mrs Thatcher   Design of Taj Mahal

3	2	5
1	4	6

6	5	2
4	3	1

The colour-frame can be used for comparing the profiles of two or more people facing the same task together, or confronting one another in argument, discussion or negotiation.

Mrs Thatcher   Ronald Reagan

3	2	5
1	4	6

5	6	3
2	1	4

Using this methodology to describe the energies of people's minds in exactly the same terms as the thinking operations required by the tasks they face, it is easier for managers to recognize both mind and task. They are using a common language for both. The result is that they can better mobilize the mental resources required so as to bring them to bear specifically and squarely on the situation facing them. The scientist, for instance, can not only optimize his energy but also get the task done as well as he is capable of doing, to the top of his ability. In that connection, it is worth exploring what happens when a scientist who is strong in green does his hard red archiving in green;

or another who prefers hard blue and hard red tries to explain and sell his project to a commercial sponsor. In some respects, through doing the task from the 'wrong approach', there could be new angles as well as consequences. The colour-frame enables you to examine such important issues simply and accurately.

The performance of an individual in making use of opportunities and resources is a function either of ability or willingness, or both. When assessing oneself or someone else it is important to separate their capability from their motivation. Using the colour-frame one can quickly make such a comparison.

Capability			Willingness		
1	3	6	5	2	1
2	4	5	6	4	3

We find that a split such as shown here is unusual. In the main people are willing to do what they are good at, and the mental muscles they like to use get stronger and stronger because they tend to be used first, last and frequently. However, when people become alerted to their capabilities and preferences we have found they are encouraged to understand more about how to increase their capability with the Thunks they tend to ignore or do not normally use effectively.

Conclusions on Thunks

In naming the Thunks we recognized them as the very design tools for the management tool-kit we had aspired to create at the outset. Because of the linguistic methods we used to find the Thunks, they were a distillation of the unconscious conceptual processes which drive thinking and which are expressed in everyday language. All the complex wisdom in the way we speak is therefore condensed in essence in each Thunk and can be unravelled by using a Thunk as a handy memory-jogger or trigger for accessing the infinite number of associations that connect to it.

In the Thunks the richness of humankind's fundamental conceptual know-how is now in a form that lends itself to conscious management of thinking for busy managers. In the following pages I hope to show you how this operates – an easier task in a live meeting than in written form since what can be conveyed verbally in a few swoops of understanding takes much longer spelled out in a book. We know that everyone operates naturally with thinking intentions, albeit mostly unconsciously. Now what previously was largely unconscious can become conscious and goal-directed. A thinking intention can be directed towards achieving a specific result.

We also conjectured, though in 1980 could not yet prove, that some thinking intentions are more often used than others. We speculated that the way people use their minds might be shaped and influenced by their education and experience in work, causing them to favour some Thunks more than others. Now in 1990, our database of thousands of managers' thinking profiles show patterns that seem significant. The Thunk Escape, for instance, is one of the least frequently used while Distinguish and Compare are among the most. By assessing large numbers of employees in specific businesses we are now getting a picture of the bias in market segments and professional groupings. This work is in its early stages, yet is proving already to be a valuable diagnostic tool for organizational and personal learning.

To conclude, the most important point of all is that the Thunks can be seen as design tools for use on anything where thinking matters. Thunks are like a set of Meccano, providing all the components needed to create any process for any task. Like any tool, they depend for their effectiveness on their user. Some will use them to make other tools. A live person, unlike any computer or machine, is capable of taking anything in his hand and turning it to his will and to his advantage at the moment. He can make a thousand tools out of a plain sheet of paper, so what can he not do with his mental resources once he can label them and see them for what they could be?

4

Conceptual Maps

With Thunks we have the basic equipment to build conceptual tools
for any occasion. The tools I build out of Thunks form three levels:
subroutines, maps and schemas of maps, and models. Altogether they
provide a range which can work well for the manager both in real-
time interchange and alone at his desk. I shall look at maps here and
in the next chapter show a map in some depth. I place a lot of
emphasis on building maps out of Thunks. As a methodology, map
building is a breakthrough, conceptualizing 'work' in the same
language as 'mind', especially the mind of the person doing the work,
because Thunks and their colours describe both mental work (task)
and mental thought (person). Parts of this chapter which describe
concepts may stretch one's grey matter somewhat. I do hope readers
will stay with me through the next pages since I have wrestled to
explain some fundamental issues for managers about conceptual
language. If you start to feel indigestion and do some skipping, then
make sure you take a good look at the figures in this chapter and the
next, to absorb images of the maps. These images will inform your
understanding of the rest of the book. If you intend to read steadily
through, please take a look at the figures now to get an immediate
sense of what maps are. For example, see Figures 4.1 and 5.1.

Since the Tower of Babel, collaboration between people using
different cognitive maps and frameworks has been an enduring
difficulty, but even when we share the same national tongue the
necessary jargon of specialism can be the very devil. It is hard to
conduct discussions across organizations in the same terms because
of the differences in meaning given to the same expressions by
different disciplines, functions and departments. The more the

shorthand of one kind of expert unites those within their domain, the more it divides them from those outside it. Yet because language itself is a principal means of development, no one can stop labelling in their own way whatever new concepts form in the mind. There are many codes that are truly international of course, including music and mathematics, science and money. We have international standards for electric wiring and road signs, rules at sea and air traffic control. One day the USA will go metric, perhaps.

There is still no language of thought process which covers everything in the same terms and is accepted by all. The laws of logic do not fit this bill, as is clear when a multi-disciplinary group find it hard to explain their rationales to one another. Part of the problem is that we do not have a common language even for the components of thought, never mind the processes that link them together. So people do not necessarily agree on the meanings or the functions of words like assumptions, options, objectives, contingencies and so on; indeed not even on the difference between data and information.

Either by sloppy wording or by loose thought construction, or just by a plain lack of conceptual grasp, managers can be observed far too often to be victims of crooked thinking, not only of other people's but of their own. They confuse, for example, the most important with the essential. It is quite possible that an objective is absolutely essential and at the same time less important than another objective that is not essential. For an operation to make profit might well be an essential goal, that is, a condition of its being allowed to continue in the business. But management might well have far more important objectives for investing in its activities. Indeed, if that part of the business were to go for maximizing its profit, the results might be disastrous for its very purpose, its *raison d'être*.

What is a Map?

I am being bold in suggesting that the Thunks could be a cross-cultural language which would enable people to decipher one another's meaning and intentions even if they use the terms goal, criterion, objective and aim interchangeably. The conceptual maps that I have developed out of Thunks, mostly to meet management concerns in large organizations, offer a visual language which breaks out of the linear trap of words. They are a description of the kinds of thinking that have to go on for a particular kind of mental task to be accomplished.

If we picture a mental task as if it were a physical job to be done on some complicated machinery, then we can imagine it would be good to have a diagram of the task or machine. Even better if the diagram could be coded with instructions about which tool is needed for each component or function, and how to use the tool as well. By analogy, the conceptual maps are just such diagrams for specific problem-types or mental tasks, coded with Thunks which show which kind of thinking tool to use when. Since a taxonomy of fundamental problem-types emerged from our analysis of management work in Philips, there is now a range of these conceptual maps on a level of abstraction that makes them quite universal and generic, so that they apply to all kinds of management, any kind of organization, and even to most situations in life. Because the Thunks were formed from a combined analysis of both human language and mental operations, when they are embodied in these conceptual maps they provide a common language to unite the task with the person. The maps join people's mental energies with the tasks they have to do.

Conceptual maps show what a task needs for it to be resolved by the person facing it, and therefore how he needs to think about it. Until I, or anyone, decide to face up to a task, I am free to use my energy as I wish but as soon as I take it up, then by definition I am responsible for doing what the task requires. I have to tune in to it and to manage my approach in such a way as to make the most efficient use of my resources. These include time, information and perhaps other people. Recognizing that another person can be the task itself, or part of the task, is key. So maps cater for people's subjective characteristics, their values, assumptions and so on, as well. When tackling a task the most important resource, of course, is one's own thinking skill and energy. While the maps aim to be objective, normative guides for thinking, their design frees the user(s) to direct skill and energy at will to any part of the map without being constrained into a sequence of thinking activities.

The idea of 'map' is so familiar and useful that it has been adopted as a metaphor for many different if perhaps related constructs. That is simply the inevitable downside of using metaphor, but then most words that are central to human experience take on many meanings, which then have to be redefined for specific purposes. This is true not only of 'map' but of 'plan' and 'task' too, which I will also define later.

A map as I describe it is a schematic word picture of the essential thought processes required for a type of task, like making a decision, developing a plan and so on. A good conceptual map is actually trying to be a blueprint for the future, generic enough in its design to be useful for many people. It derives from the analysis and distillation of accumulated experience on the particular type of task it addresses. From these sources, it defines some absolute minimum conditions that have to be met in one's thought process. The signposts or steps in the map show you the way to go with your thinking, so that the task will be addressed both soundly and thoroughly. My maps provide soundness through structure, and thoroughness through questions that ensure you will think up all that is needed to handle the task. Because a map identifies the crucial elements of its task, anyone who omits to cover them all is risking failure.

Each element or step in the map directs the search for information that will be relevant and essential for success in dealing with the situation. The questions are process questions, open rather than closed. In other words, the map will not tell you what the answers should be, only the kind of question or the kind of answer. Although no map can guarantee that the right answers will be forthcoming, what it can do is to warn that some questions have not yet been answered. The questions it asks create, figuratively speaking, empty data-bins, so that you notice when these have not been filled. In short, what I mean when I talk of a map is a structured visual layout of questions on a piece of paper (or in a computer) that focus your thinking to achieve a desired goal, however loosely framed the goal might be.

By contrast, a thinking plan is a route with order or sequence in it that you personally work out for a particular situation based on a map. Maps have no sequence, they just spread the territory out in front of you, so you need to plan the sequence of your way through them. Of course you can make a plan without using a map. A thinking plan rarely has any pretences to be an object-lesson for future events but rather is made on the spot to deal with an immediate difficulty. It is situational and, in the hurly-burly of argument or the pressure of events, can sometimes be formulated on the very edge of panic. But this is far from a necessary condition. Wise managers are more likely to make a plan for thinking ahead to avoid the dangers of being forced to react inadequately, starting fires that they later have to put out. Managers who are too busy are often those who have failed to think things through in advance, and so have plenty on their hands. It is so obvious that an ounce of anticipation is worth a ton of activity and yet it is common to deal with uncertainty by 'going in on a wing and a prayer' and relying on one's wits. Luckily, 20 per cent of planning usually produces 80 per cent of results, so that the back of an envelope can take us a long way. Good old Pareto.

On many pages in this book the word 'task' crops up. Integrally bound up with my concept of maps, it is a convenient jargon word, nice and short, to denote any situation that is important and difficult enough to require one's best thinking. Although most tasks would appear to be one-off events, this is only true of the actual circumstances and the people involved, the issues and all the information about them: the data if you like. It is because these are unique or unfamiliar that the task is difficult. However, at the level of process, all situations can be classified into types, according to the kinds of thinking they require for their successful and economical handling. A task for instance that people constantly face is to determine what to do first when too many things are crowding in. Every busy person with some control over their time sets priorities, probably several times a day. This is a generalizable 'task' because, although the items to choose between are always different or shifting, there is a common thought process that can always be replicated. Isn't it odd that with all the practice people get, many cannot handle this task of setting priorities well? This is because practice makes perfect only when you can observe what you do against some yardstick so as to change if necessary. To provide a kind of yardstick is one of the functions of a map. A map sets standards.

You can imagine a whole system of tasks, a whole system of maps, with interconnecting elements and overlaps, but revealing the real differences between the way that you should handle one situation from another. Because of the infinite complexity and variety of thought, it would be unrealistic to expect a perfect taxonomy, forever fixed, but one could certainly expect there to be several levels in such task-maps, and probably some form of hierarchy in them. Such a hierarchy might consist simply of the range from very high level, abstract, and universalist concepts to low level, concrete and specific expressions of them.

In my work with Philips, we did come up with various map configurations, until we realized that it was not good enough to treat maps as some kind of static architecture, except for a particular purpose or situation. It does make sense to go firm on a model, to freeze the frame and hold it still for long enough to make use of doing so. Yet maps, like the mind that makes them, are essentially organic and dynamic. What is fundamental in one map can be peripheral in another. What is at the highest level of abstraction in one map can perform a small function in another. For example, specifying the information available is of core importance when discovering why something has gone wrong, but it may be less on another task like making a change, which is bound to make much of the detailed information irrelevant. To take another example, being clear about one's values is critical for design or prescription, but worse than useless in diagnosis. Much depends on the task. The difficulty is knowing what the task is. This is one of the key points I want to make about the language of maps. Most managers do not have a common language through which they can recognize what kind of task they are facing. What one manager means by 'make a plan' is quite different from another's meaning. With maps the concept behind the task is opened out in one quick visual image so that people can agree whether they are facing a task that is planning, decision-making, selling or what.

In order to illustrate some of the points I have been making, I show below a list of generic labels that could be titles of maps. Beside each one is the sort of question managers are always asking themselves.

	Map	**Typical management questions**
1	Recognition	WHAT's facing me?
2	Orientation	WHERE am I in this problem/situation?
3	Priority	HOW SOON should I tackle each issue?
4	Information	WHAT SORT of information is worth gathering?
5	Decision	WHICH option should I choose now?
6	Evaluation	WHY does something matter?
7	Evaluation	WHY ought this to work?
8	Prediction	WHAT MIGHT happen?
9	Plan	HOW might my decision be implemented?
10	Learning	HOW might I benefit from experience?
11	Persuasion	HOW could (s)he be influenced?
12	Creation	HOW ELSE might we do it?
13	Diagnosis	WHY did that go off-course?
14	Delegation	HOW WELL should the project be done?

15	Delegation	WHO may decide WHAT, WHERE, WHEN?
16	Quantification	HOW MUCH, HOW MANY?
etc . . .		

All of these tasks are probably recognizable and familiar to everyone reading these pages and you will notice that they are not all on the same level. This list is just a sample. Whatever the labels used in the left-hand column, the questions on the right are meat and drink for every problem-solver. Incidentally, the word 'problem' is significant by its absence. This is because it is a nice example of management vocabulary that is so loose that it is unusable as proper jargon. 'Problem' is used variously to mean: an impending disaster, a mess, a variance from course or a cause to be found, a decision to be made, a feeling of being lost or out of control, in short almost anything you could call a task.

By way of an aside, in the list above, those six great Anglo-Saxon words so celebrated by Kipling are made to stand out in capitals, not just because they are part of the stock-in-trade of many a specialist, but also to emphasize their tremendous range and how useful they are. This list of tasks was not actually derived from the famous serving men, though conceivably they could have been because the six are such generic tools. In fact, the list on the left describes the tasks for which the Philips team have made maps. Every one of the sixteen tasks needs to be thought through differently. Use a process suitable for one task on another, and you court disaster. The exceptions to that bleak statement are of course the overlaps and commonalities that can be found. There is, for example, a strong affinity between setting priorities and making decisions. On the other hand, the task of developing a plan is quite different from that involved when making a choice, though this is by no means obvious because they can actually both be led by the question 'How shall we do it?' This is where managers go astray when they are talking to each other. The same question can imply quite different thinking processes. A decision requires the rejection of all options and the commitment to one single option at one moment in time. As Solomon realized, you cannot have two natural mothers of one baby. Whereas planning how to launch a new product on to the market in two years' time requires you to keep as many options open as possible, changing and steering the plan as

CONCEPTUAL MAPS

you go through time, only staying firm on the launch itself, the ultimate goal. What can be confusing about this is that over those two years many decisions will have to be made *en route*. But the process used on each of these decisions within the plan will be a decision map, not a planning one.

With such complexity, how can everyone agree, unless they have a common way of mapping, a common map of maps? Everyone has a different world-view. We all have different constructs of reality, our perceptions are coloured by diverse values, assumptions, connotations, associations, sensations and language, in fact all that is within each person including their experiences. Psychology now has a discipline called cognitive mapping which charts a person's world-view. I want to make it plain at once that conceptual mapping is quite different. Basically, cognitive mapping is about data, the items, memories, images and values thàt are unique to each person. Conceptual mapping is about process, that is, how you seek data, how you turn it into information, how you use it to help reach conclusions. It will be noticed that all sixteen maps listed above are to help you conclude what to do. In so-called cognitive maps all the data is expected to be changing and different between people; and it should be. In what I am calling conceptual maps, the process is expected to be stable and common to all; or should be. No two people will share the same cognitive map. A group of people, in fact a whole organization, can share the same conceptual map.

Precision in the use of language, or lack of it, critically affects the way people form conceptual maps in their heads. For example, there are two tasks on the list above concerning Evaluation, and their related questions in both cases start with 'Why?'. Yet those 'Whys' are quite different in purpose. Number 6, 'Why something matters' (to a person or an assessor or a market), can be seen as an essentially subjective kind of evaluation, based on chosen or adopted criteria; I would say soft blue. Number 7, 'Why something ought to work' (because it follows sound principles of cause-effect relationship and probability), can be seen as an essentially objective kind of evaluation, based on inference from the facts; I would say hard blue. Yet who is to say that evaluation is not a proper word for both functions? All of the sixteen listed tasks above can in fact be expressed in quite different ways, simply by manipulating the various functions of words such as 'why' and 'how'. For instance, changing the verb enables the word 'how' to include:

Priority (3)   How shall I order my time, first and then?
Decision (5)   How should I do it?
Plan (9)   How will I make it happen, first this, then that?
Diagnosis (13)   How did that happen?

If language can be so flexible how can the manager distinguish which of the four above is meant when the boss says 'How shall we do this?' A lot of breath is wasted between people sorting out what is meant in a simple phrase. And even then they don't.

Just to polish things off here, 'Where, When, How much' and even 'What' can be subsumed under 'How?' There are levels even in the famous six. Of course there are. When it comes to language things are always complex.

You may well be thinking that you would add other questions to the list of sixteen. There could be a map of innovation or one on negotiation or one about managing risk. Some of the sixteen could be grouped with one another in various ways, and all the sixteen tasks are clearly not of the same order of magnitude. All this is true. This list is not a taxonomy. I wanted to show a tangible list to illustrate some key points and to establish two major needs. First managers need a 'problem' vocabulary which they share, and second even with such a vocabulary, thinking is better done with the support of pictures, that is schematic maps of words such as are shown in this chapter and the next.

'Problem' Vocabulary

First the 'problem' vocabulary issue. The lack of agreement about what words mean is almost as bad as the chaos of different languages brought about to ensure that the Tower of Babel could never achieve success. Here is a random sample of words jotted down from a couple of management workshops where real problems were being actively dealt with:

A
monitor   political   feasibility   commonsense
    persuasion   difference   threats   authorization
achievement   planning   fun   effort   resources
    responsibility   credibility   impact   co-ordination
test   ideas   analysis   power   motivate   care
         cost/benefit   success   objective   risk
    goal   creativity   practicality   failure

B

events   reasons   challenge   level   scope   actions
    impressions   relevance   risk/threat   options
    intuition   conclusion   cause   decision   outcome
experience   rationale   test   categories
    experiment   values   hypothesis   search   relations
    description   analysis   activities   assumption
construct   opinion   constraint   inference   analogy
    comparison   similar   facts   statement
    probability   problem   opportunity   crisis

Nothing strange about such terms, you might say. Yet it is the diverse meanings assigned that matter. Arguments that in the end boil down to different perceptions of, say, goal and objective lose all credibility in the telling. It can take managers an hour and a lot of blood to reach clarity on the difference between an assumption and a criterion. Why does this matter? Not because anyone has the right to dictate what use people make of words, but because no one has the right! It matters either because the people concerned are not thinking clearly or because they are actually not even thinking straight.

The difficulty hardly occurs when those managers share the same conceptual map, because it is not the words that matter but their conceptual functions. Who cares if my criterion is his objective, is her motive, or other people's goal, factor, parameter, yardstick, or constraint? Everyone should care if they agree that the words are interchangeable and if by doing so they miss the significance of any conceptual differences between them. Whatever the words used, the soundness of the real-life outcome will be under threat if the meaning of the live information and its relationship with other information cannot be held still, looked at and evaluated with consistency. For instance, is your meaning of the word parameter an absolute boundary, a 'must' in fact, or is it closer to a criterion which might or might not be essential? For many otherwise able people, it seems that thoughts and process constructs are whirling around in the mind, randomly, unrecognizably, and without any apparent constancy. In such conditions, how can anyone achieve the human equivalent of a printer's registration? How can anyone navigate when suffering the combination of being in space without landmarks and having only an erratically gyrating compass? Only some form of spatial mapping can enable one to progress with any confidence or with ease, economy and effectiveness.

A solution might be to try to force people in an organization to use a common set of terms rigidly defined so that they all speak the same jargon. This solution does not appeal to me, first because it can stultify imagination exactly where it is most needed – in management, and second because it is impossible to achieve. What I propose is freedom in language at the spoken level, but the discipline of Thunks and maps underpinning language so that conceptual understanding is assured.

Visual Mapping

A geographical atlas is full of maps of different scale. A map of Europe will be preceded by a smaller-scale map of the world and larger-scale maps of its countries, and then their provinces, and so on. This function of level (you may recognize the Thunk) must apply also to the maps we make of our conceptual world. There are maps upon maps and maps within maps. I have tried to illustrate this in Figure 4.1, called a schema of maps, which is not attempting to cover all of thinking by any means, but just the general area of 'achieving something new'.

The purpose of this figure is to show some key relationships between various conceptual aspects of the mega task of New Achievement. It offers signposts from one map to another, and invites you to make connections with other maps that might be relevant. It is schematic at a very high level of simplicity, with simple words and phrases to sum up what is involved in each step. It goes without saying for the purposes of fitting into the space of a book that the Thunks detail of these maps has been taken out. (The map, named Orientation, in Figure 5.2, gives Thunks details.) The main driving-force colour of each step in the maps is represented in shape codes. Thus in the New Achievement Super-Map, Create Ideas is elliptical and hence green; Develop Ideas and Communicate are hexagonal and hence red; Sell Ideas and Judge, Buy and Use Ideas are both rectangular and hence blue. I use the phrase 'driving force' and this should be explained briefly although it is an extremely important concept in terms of directing your mind. One of the characteristics of thinking is that, unless it is on some narrow and specialist front, any task will always demand the use of all the colours. People whose thinking styles show them to have but little of one colour are thereby severely handicapped some of the time. But for any part of a task, there is usually one colour that is more essential than the others, the driving force. By the shapes code, or by colouring a map, you can tell at a glance which colour, that is which Super-Thunk, is driving each step. This enables you immediately to identify in which direction you will broadly need to send your mind at each stage. A quick comparison between the New Achievement Super-Map and Real Creativeness shows the green Thunks will be driving the latter much more than the former, which in itself is a commentary on the overall drive of New Achievement. When handling Real Creativeness then it would be valuable to ensure that your team had plenty of green energy, while moving to the Selling map requires more soft red and blue.

The schema in Figure 4.1 shows that in bringing about a new achievement, you had better do something at least about each of the six elements of the super-map. If you organize no system to Plan and Control your progress, this is liable to be a severe weakness and your project might even fail. So the super-map connects with a map that shows how to Develop a Plan. Due to space constraints what is not shown on the schema is that Develop a Plan has its own mini-maps or sub-assemblies or subroutines. There are whole rafts of management techniques for mini-maps, like network analysis or PERT, which would be used for example, in the red step Reorganize. The idea of mini-maps is made visible in the map Real Creativeness, where the green step Change What Is points towards three specific ways to do this, with the three named green mini-maps, Challenge Assumptions, Change Perception and Play with Means/Ends. Such tools can be built into all parts of every map.

All the elements of all the maps in the schema have been created out of Thunks. As I will explain in Chapter 6 you can build your own maps for anything, by putting the right Thunks together into suitable runs, clusters and configurations. In the account of the schema that follows, I hope you will catch glimpses of the Thunks that are operating at each stage, and to help I will mention them explicitly here and there. For a detailed look at a map with Thunks I have included the map Orientation in the next chapter.

The schema in Figure 4.1 was originally designed for a programme of work in the National Westminster Bank which has been running since 1985. The bank is developing a more creative approach to the markets, which demands greater flexibility in the services it produces,

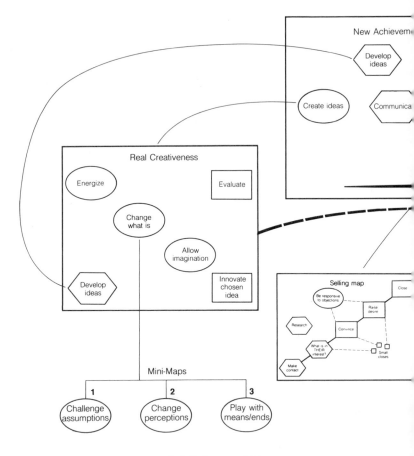

4.1 Schema of Maps

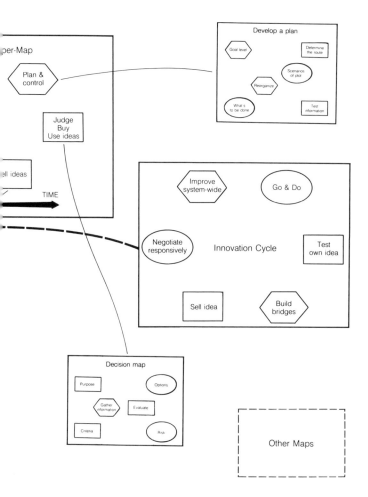

per-Map

Plan & control

Judge
Buy
Use ideas

ell ideas

TIME

Develop a plan

Goal level

Determine the route

Scenarios of plot

Reorganize

What's to be done

Test information

Innovation Cycle

Improve system-wide

Go & Do

Negotiate responsively

Test own idea

Sell idea

Build bridges

Decision map

Purpose

Options

Gather information

Evaluate

Criteria

Risk

Other Maps

delivers and supports. Big changes are being brought in over several years, which have been assisted by Creative Problem-Solving Workshops on which maps are used. The aim of these workshops, conceived by Ron Jackson, former Director of Training at the Nat West Staff College, is to enlarge the thinking of managers in certain parts of the bank in the following way. The solid, safe and bureaucratic culture that used to be a feature of clearing banks and still has real validity, is led by the blue Super-Thunk, Judgement, on which it is traditional for lenders to pride themselves. Into this style of working the Bank wants to bring creative skills, led by the green Super-Thunk Realise. These new thinking skills will then have to flourish amid the normal ways of operating (Judgement) and against much of the experience of those concerned. (Experience is found mostly in the red Super-Thunk Describe. So Ron and I are teaching the managers first how to operate in creative green mode with mini-maps of Thunks such as Challenge Assumptions, Re-describe and Escape, and then how to bridge the gulf from green to the blue analytical modes of the environment they work in.

I will unbundle the schema in Figure 4.1 here to show how it covers a whole range of thinking activities which lead through to achieving something new. The schema reads from left to right, so first you need to open up to ideas. Even sensible banking personnel can be encouraged to venture into the soft green Thunks of Pretend and Symbolise. But in the end the more far-out these are, for instance Unform and Feel, the harder it is for others to accept them. Especially if those who must accept are firmly grounded in the need for evidence (red) and hard red numbers, or if they employ the rigorous probability of the Thunk Test at a too early stage. What is necessary is that you keep the creation of ideas quite separate in your mind from innovating them, and tackle them quite differently at different stages as the maps show. There is a strong dotted line connecting Real Creativeness and the Innovation Cycle. This is to symbolize the bridge that must be built between getting ideas and implementing them. The bridge is strengthened at both ends and in the middle with maps, and this notion underlies the particular configuration of maps in the schema.

Let me explain with an example. Somebody in a moment of thought with green Escape conceived the brilliant idea of buying up the Third World debts owing to other banks throughout the western world. Of course the terms have to make the prospect attractive to all concerned, but the banks have been very busy reducing their dependence on the repayment of these loans, to the extent that they have almost assumed the burden that is theoretically on the shoulders of the debtor countries. So some banks might well be glad to sell. It would depend on their criteria (Value). The question is, how could the buying-up bank make a return on its gamble? You might imagine that when the debt-buying idea was first mooted the response to the question of return on the gamble would be put as a condemning blue judgement 'How on earth can that do us any good?' rather than as a genuine request for red information 'How can that do us good?' Brilliant ideas need a lot of development under the auspices of Develop Ideas before they should be championed even by their proposers. Information must be sought (Observe, Specify, Categorise), many avenues explored (Look in/out) and experiments made, with results that can be observed and measured and used as feedback (Compare). Getting an idea can be very fast. Giving it legs enough to stand means work. So the stage of developing ideas in the Real Creativeness map is driven by red information-gathering and try-outs, though of course there will also be green to think up and Pursue possible modifications and blue to judge which are worth following up (Interpret and Predict). If a good job is done in developing the idea so that it is robust and viable, at least the entry onto the bridge is firm and strong. The thing ought to work (Test), the idea might fly. The originator at least can Commit to it.

In fact, the Real Creativeness map shows within itself that a powerful thrust (in green) will come up against the evaluation process (blue) sooner or later. There will be no chance of innovating the idea if this screening is not positive. It is essential to so manage things that a good idea does not get nipped in the bud too early, when it is not grown enough to survive. This might also suggest to would-be innovators that they had better be clear about the basis on which their ideas will be evaluated. For instance in what goal context (Set Level and Look in/out) and with what criteria (Value)? Possibly the bank will currently be more concerned with Eastern Europe than with Brazil, or in various ways the demands of the idea on capital will come up against even larger opportunities; and what will it do to share prices (Predict)? It is obviously wise to know the context of strategic objectives in which their own project is liable to be competing.

The opposite end of the bridge cannot be strengthened enough simply by testing out the validity and feasibility of the new idea before exposing it to the approvers. Even if the idea is sound, is the environment suitable and ready to receive it? An idea is often ahead of its time, and always feels so if it is exceptional. The syndrome is rather like the balance between technology push and market pull. It was once thought that the only successful new products would be those invited by market pull. Closer investigation shows that this is by no means the case, and that real winners are apt to be ahead (Realise) of the felt needs or wants (Interpret and Value) of the marketplace. Think of the Xerox copier. To overcome this approver inertia or even active resistance, one has to plan a campaign for bringing in anything new to the organization.

Ideas need harbingers. Things must be got going, milestones established in the calendar and influential people recognized (Distinguish). Some of this could be started, on a contingency basis, even before the idea itself is fully ready to go public. The risk of this advance effort proving to be a waste, because the idea turns out not to be viable enough, is worth it. The cost of an idea is tiny at the outset and swells exponentially at each successful passing through its approval hurdles. Much of this cost is opportunity cost, including what benefits are lost by delay. As soon as any idea looks promising, it is worth getting into advance action on the innovation cycle by strengthening the far end of the bridge.

Most of the middle section of the bridge is to do with communication (Describe). People cannot support an idea they know nothing about. They must be informed. Yet completely adequate information is hardly ever enough to secure the achievement of something new, because it is sure to displace something old. Customs, habits and levels of comfort enjoyed because of familiarity will be upset. Some people will feel they no longer know where they are (Interpret) and begin to be threatened by uncertainty (Predict). Worse still, they might not like the change (Value), whether in itself or for fear of loss of power. And of course they must be convinced it is a sound proposition (Test) as well as wanting to give it their full-blooded Commitment. In short they have to buy the idea as well as know about it.

This is the role of the selling map, which has a strong interface of course with the map of decision. When S is selling an idea to B, B as the buyer is the one who will come to judgement and make a decision yes or no. If S bears this in mind, playing into the decision process of the potential approver, it helps the right decision to emerge, whether yea or nay. In a sense therefore the map of choosing can be seen also as a map for selling as well as one for buying. On the other hand, just as to make a presentation is not an identical process to persuasion so it is useful to see both the similarity and the difference between the processes of selling and of decision.

This rough survey of the schema has been done not with completeness in mind but to offer a means of insight into how the maps relate and overlap, and how the 25 Thunks act as interchangeable common components at a more specific level. You could almost say that any map could be treated as a mini-map or subroutine of another map. This chapter has so far reviewed mapping from the top down. I will walk through the whole of a single map in some depth in the next chapter and in the one following I will show how to build maps from the bottom up.

The Use of Thinking Energy

When it comes to thinking, energy can be as important as skill. This is because it is so intensely personal a matter. When someone does not feel like thinking in a particular way, it may be such hard work to try that he will not make the best use of himself. This goes farther than the age-old dilemma of the 'creative' artist or writer or scientist, who often has to discipline himself to get down to it, rather than whistle in the wind for inspiration. No, it is a common experience for every manager that he does not want to deal with a problem the way that his colleagues are steering, and he gets frustrated at the way they are wasting time and not getting at the heart of the matter. Alternatively, working at his own desk, he may 'know' that he should be following one line of attack, yet what he feels is something like 'Damned if I will!' So what do you do if the map says 'do this with your mind' and you don't want to?

I advocate maps as tools that are under the control of their user, not the other way round. Some thinking routines are supposed to be followed strictly, step by step in the right order and nothing left out. This is specially true of logical procedures which might be threatened by some apparently non-rational approach, or where a systematic discipline is the only way to ensure thoroughness. In the kind of map proposed in this book, the chunks of thinking that must be considered are identified, so that you realize the consequences of ignoring them.

But precisely how you tackle each step, for how long and in what detail is elastic. There is no sequence. This is the message of laying out the maps not as sequenced steps or stages but as elements in a system. One can start anywhere and go anywhere. Of course there will sometimes be a natural flow, or a natural end point, but the decision is the user's. Freedom is designed into the maps as far as possible so that if you don't feel like 'it' now you can switch to another part of the map to do some useful thinking there.

Most people's thinking is driven by feeling anyway. There is a tendency for people to think the kind of thinking they feel like, whatever the situation. Anyhow, they have only a hazy idea that there could be any other way to think. Although they see there are options in the actions to take as a result of thinking, they do not begin to realize there are options to the way they might think about it. Maps enable you to recognize where your 'favourite' thinking crops up, how you cling to that because it is easy for you and how you may well ignore large chunks of a problem's needs because you just don't like the kind of thinking it demands. We all do it. I dislike some aspects of the red Thunks and love the green. My wife is tremendous with blue ones. When we are working together we consciously try to monitor ourselves as we both have a tendency to let red slip between us. It is really quite amusing to see us both bolster each other up to get our red Thunks going – it really takes an effort of mental will to turn your mind to the parts of maps you usually don't reach.

Of course you don't know what you think until you have said it or written it. Even if I am trying to think in a red direction I might find myself skirting off into green or blue. With practice, with the maps as guides, the quality of the different kinds of thinking that each colour and Thunk requires becomes almost tangible. As you start your thinking you can tell if you are in Specify, or Escape, or Test. Even the body language feels different. Some people feel they actually access different Thunks in different areas of their minds so they almost physically send their thinking to the place where Value is, where Symbolise is, where Code is. Thunks are the name for what you intend with your mind and they put a label on an attribute of consciousness which as yet is not recognized in mainstream psychology. For the most part people are only conscious of where they have already been with their minds, not where they are going. Until you can pictorialize your potential thoughts on a complex situation in some diagrammatic shorthand either inside your head or on to paper you cannot expect to 'intend' with your thinking process. With the maps you have intentional guidelines and a marvellous insight into the nature of the problems you must address.

Why Maps?

The most common way in which people reflect what is going on in their heads is through lists and hierarchies. Everyone jots down a list in a hurry to guide their thinking. The trouble with a list is that it is one damn thing after another. In order to give it shape and significance people may then sequence the list, relating and numbering items, shifting them around into an order that better reflects how they want to attack the problem. Even so, if list format persists, with subcategories and sub-subs, as the British Civil Service reports so elegantly do it, it is still difficult to see the relationships between items in other parts of the list.

If you turn your list into a map, you instantly improve your thinking tool. Ease of memory, significance of relationship, differentiation of meaning between items, flexibility of sequence, are aided by the map. In general terms the idea of mapping is well known in management literature and probably most usefully covered in Tony Buzan's excellent book *Use your Head* (BBC Publications, 1974). The maps described in this book are somewhat different from Buzan's mind-mapping. Buzan maps are content or answer maps, which depend upon your thinking up and asking yourself the necessary questions to handle a task. The special feature of the maps in this book is that questions are built into them. They show you the way to go with your thinking, so that the task will be thoroughly addressed. These maps provide the structure and links that ensure you will think up all that is needed to handle the task. This is possible because the maps are pure process, and at a high level truly generic so they can be used whatever the situation or circumstances.

When I watch managers using this mapping technology in meetings I see its practical value. They can share a common set of maps, which helps them to clear their lines, and agree what they really must cover between them in the short time they have in which to work. They can select what they need and cross refer from one map to another to join their thinking through a common path. They may appear to work for stretches at a time without reference directly to a map, but then periodically they will focus on one to check off what they have done, what they have ignored and shouldn't, and what they want to do next. These maps are silent, wise facilitators, unobtrusively waiting to be consulted when necessary. The maps may be placed on the table, pinned on the wall, but more often they are drawn up from memory on the flip chart at crucial moments. In cramped, hurried conditions, in a car, a railway station buffet or an airport lounge, a map can be quickly jotted on a paper napkin or railway timetable. Working alone, people can use a map without any feeling of constraint by the presence of other people. They can gain experience using them, developing their personal standards of thinking which then feed into meetings. Some managers are now inputting maps into their personal computers and lap-tops for ready reference.

In the flux of business today, when there is little certainty to depend upon, the maps provide a certain method of plotting your path through the commercial jungle. One of the central pushes behind our original research was the growing concern in Philips at the increasing uncertainty in business. This was detected in 1977! Thirteen years on, the world is a far more uncertain place commercially. The maps are needed even more than when we first conceived them. At the simplified level in the schema in Figure 4.1 the maps can be memorized and referred to when the situation is desperate or you are confused, just as people refer to the schematic map of the four points of the compass if lost out on the moors, or otherwise all at sea.

Fortunately our minds operate like video discs, rather than sequential video tapes, so we have immediate access to any part of any map without delay. The spatial layout of these interconnected maps makes ready access possible, both for searching for the right map and then making progress through the chosen one. Man has the specific ability to multiply his capacity by changing the level on which he decides to be operating at any one moment. He can switch mentally from buying a grape to a bunch, to bunches of bunches, to a vine, to a vineyard, to a whole year's vintage in a microsecond. Since all information arranges itself in hierarchies, he can equally switch from the smallest detail to the top of any pyramid of concepts, and back again. While the computer operates in millions of instructions per second and the brain at only 126 per second, the apparently slow human can swoop through levels, dimensions and directions that give him a short-cutting advantage as it were many times the speed of light. By a change of insight, he makes galaxies of calculation irrelevant and redundant. He is the master of his own zoom lens, the pilot of his own mental helicopter, the one who determines how wide are his horizons, how long the lever he uses to lift the world, how close the gearing between his task and his sources of power and force.

The fruitful use of maps depends upon recognizing conceptually the kind of problem you are facing in order to select the map you will use. If you cannot recognize what kind of map you want, then you need a means whereby you can sort one out. We have developed a map to do this which we call Orientation. Because this is such a vital map, upon which the whole edifice of your processes of thinking depend, I have detailed it in some depth in the next chapter.

5

Where the Hell am I?

The proper name for this map is Orientation, chosen to carry all the implications that are around at the moment when we stop and think. Actually 'Where the hell am I?' is more usually muttered under the breath when thinking has come to a full stop, paralysed, frustrated, going round in circles, repeating thoughts that go nowhere, under increasing stress. 'Why do I feel so impotent, so incompetent and useless?' The pulse-rate rises in desperation, or energy sinks into the slough of despond and misery. Meanwhile time marches on relentless, and the situation is worsening.

Conceptual mapping is the art of putting questions to yourself. In this chapter, to examine the art in some depth, I will go into just one map, Orientation, Figure 5.1, the art of knowing where you are and which way to point. 'What's facing me and what should I do about it?' are the everyday questions of every person who is mentally alert. The purpose of taking up and using a map of orientation is simply to raise confidence enough to go forward with a suitable plan for thinking, so that a conclusion can be reached that will be acted upon. Use it only when you feel lost, when the situation may feel so unclear you do not even know how to think about it, even how to get started. It is this uncomfortable kind of situation which calls for some formalization of the natural processes of situational awareness. The moment you know where you are and the direction to point yourself in, worry about awareness has vanished. Abandon the map at once, until perhaps the fog of uncertainty comes down again later on. This map is for someone who wants and needs to be aware of his thinking, and so be in control. In this sense it can claim to be a rather central map.

The basic purpose of orientation is to lead you to the thinking map

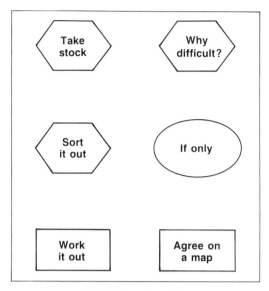

5.1 Orientation Map

or tool which is most apt for the situation. It causes you to ask yourself:

> What needs to be done, what stops you, and why?
> In which direction should you turn your mind?
> Where or at what stage of the whole process are you?
> On what level of detail is it worth tackling the issue?
> and so on.

Although it is a case of stop now to think, the purpose is to encourage your thinking onwards constructively, so that you can take the right action. Because orientation is about the thinking-action that must precede physical action, it invites you to look dispassionately at the information you have and haven't got. Is it the answers you lack or are you unable even to find the questions? If you know the questions, it is easy to go and get the answers, but if you don't then you'd better grope and struggle towards the map that will supply you with the right kinds of question.

Key to this awareness is the need to face up to the two different halves of any situation and find a way through to action which will resolve both. One half is the external objective reality of the world outside. When this excites your attention, it presents a problem or an opportunity in the form of some change or other. Something's up which seems to deserve action in the world. The other half of the situation is the internal subjective feeling of discomfort this 'something' is giving you. For some reason, what has excited your attention fails to trigger any useful response. You do not know what to do about it nor even how to begin your thinking. Your inner mind is full of anxiety, frustration, fear of blind alleys or wild-goose chasing. You may not even know what kind of difficulty it is that you feel. Simply, you are stuck.

Orientation is a way of bringing together and resolving these internal and external aspects of reality. In Figure 5.2 the questions that probe into the external are on the left and on the right are the internal. It's no use saying that one is more important than another. If the external problem should disappear but I still feel uncomfortable about it, the real problem is not solved. You will undoubtedly recall cases of a colleague or friend who felt he had solved a problem while all about him the world is caving in. The promotion of a manager to some other division is sometimes only just in time to save his reputation. *Après lui le déluge.*

The Orientation Map

The nature of orientation is especially and essentially individual. This is a map for clarifying what is thoroughly obscure, otherwise you have no need of it. I have chosen this map as an example of what can sometimes be done even in endemically unpromising conditions! I shall walk through the outline map in slow motion. The detail of each step will be spelled out showing the main Thunks involved. Then I will make some narrative illustration. My reasoning is that once you have got the hang of each step, the economy of the full map, one whole picture on one spread, will become obvious as in Figure 5.2. The danger of my descriptive approach is that it could lead to the impression that the steps on maps should be handled sequentially. People rarely plan the sequence of their own thought, never mind dictate the sequence for anyone else, especially because of the need for frequent recycling and feed-forward as well as feedback. When working with this map, or any map for that matter, the layout of the steps provides you with potential stepping stones, which you can jump on to or not at will. A further point on the economy of these maps, impossible to illustrate in black and white, is the colour-coding, embodied in the Thunks. If you can bring yourself to mark the maps in this book, then run highlighter pens (blue, red and green) over the maps to reveal the colour-coding. (See Figure 3.1 for the colour and shape codes.)

Step 1   Stop and Take Stock

Observe: WHAT'S UP?
Compare: How does what actually happens (performance) compare with what should happen (standards)?
Specify: How (much) have standards or performance changed?
Interpret: Does it require and is it worth more thinking?

Serious thinking begins when something makes us stop what we are doing. 'What's up?' we ask. One speaks of attention being 'arrested'. We slow down or stop what was proceeding in case of error or lost opportunity. We stop and think. What to focus on? Something must have changed for us to notice something and to be concerned about it. A difference can be discovered between what is actually happening and what should be. It may at present be unclear whether this is due to a change in actual events or a change in our own standards and expectations. But when we compare what should be happening with what actually is, there is some discrepancy.

As I write I am aware of some dissatisfaction with my computer. Is it really getting slower than it should be? Has its performance gone down from what it was? Or do I now expect a faster reaction time because since buying it my standards have gone up? Maybe it is because my publisher needs this manuscript soon, so I am just temporarily impatient. Perhaps it is just as good as when I bought it, but if I see the possibilities of these new machines, then I feel dissatisfaction just the same. The thinking-action I should take will depend on whether this is a matter of change in performance or in standards. If performance has gone down, then I should find the cause for this before choosing the best remedy. If my standards have gone up, I might consider what to buy instead, and whether the change would be worth it.

If the matter is this simple it is fairly easy to proceed. Yet often managers face problems without being clear about the discrepancy before them, because they do not know one or other of the key answers, either the level of performance or the standard required.

Take stock

WHAT'S UP?

How does what *actually* happens (performance) compare with what *should* happen (standards)?

How (much) have standards or performance changed?

Does it require and is it worth more thinking?

Sort it out

HAVE WE GOT THE RIGHT PROBLEM?

What other aspects, parts or kinds of the problem are there?

What connections or separations should be made?

What aspects are fixed? What's critical?

Are there priorities?

Work it out

WHAT APPROACH WILL MATCH THE PROBLEM NOW?

Which map is ready made and suitable?

Organise all the aspects of the process

Make a map that suits yourself

5.2 Thunks Orientation Map

Why is this difficult to think about?

ℭ WHAT KIND OF DIFFICULTY DO I FEEL?

ℭ Is it about information or process?

ꓱ Should I look into the problem or outside it, or at myself?

ᴍ How far is it *my* problem? When could others help?

If only

ꓘ WE WOULD BE UNSTUCK, IF ONLY . . . . .

ꓘ We had more confidence in our information

ꓘ OR we could challenge assumptions and reach a new idea

ꓘ OR we could strike a balance between competing values

The map we'll use: commitment

ᴍ IS THIS THE WAY TO GO? DOES THE PROCESS SUIT

ᴍ Are we (all) committed?

ꓔ How and when will we take stock of progress?

ᗡ Where on our map shall we start?

Sometimes, this is because the information is difficult to get but sometimes because they have not even asked the questions. It is perfectly possible to have a vague feeling of unease without being able to make an accurate and specific subtraction sum between what should be and what actually pertains, and this unease could be authentic. Everywhere we look in public affairs today we see lack of such information. Do you know whether or not your water is safe to drink? Is it a sensible risk now to swim at Something-on-Sea? How much, if any, damage is being invisibly inflicted on the health of the nation by the intrusion of alien substances into manufactured food? What about the spraying of crops and the feeding of animals? In this area of concern, food and drink, there are many more such questions to raise. Yet in all cases the knowledge or agreement on 'what should be' and 'what is' can not be ascertained. On the other hand, the level of anxiety in the public mind is growing and certainly authentic.

This leads us to the last question to ask when taking stock. Does our concern require more thinking and is an investment in thinking worth it? Clearly if the person concerned does not care enough about the gratuitous insertion of products like milk, sugar and soya into foods where one would not naturally expect them, then he should not waste time thinking about it. The subject is not a real concern – for him. Alternatively, he might feel that there is nothing at all he can do about it, and so although it does concern him, he won't think about it more than he can help. Thinking is for reaching conclusions, and while to have reached a conclusion is in itself a blessed state, it will still leave him dissatisfied unless and until his conclusion can lead to action. So ask what changes are outside your control or influence, and what changes do you fear. Observe the situation facing you and discover how long it has lasted so far, and what changed (just) before it arose. Even try for first thoughts on what you could probably do. If you do not feel that action is worth trying, consider what you'll do to improve those tentative first thoughts.

Nonetheless people do invest in thinking with only the remotest chance of resolving their issue in successful action. If they do manage to achieve some effective action, they probably will have identified some intermediate think-goal which has been reached. From the example above, if someone concludes that it's worth finding out only the level at which dairy products are likely to begin to do him more harm than good, then his think-goal is simply to discover a standard for himself. This is an intermediate goal only, and will scarcely revolutionize the food manufacturing industry overnight! Nor will it either diminish or increase his concern, until he also works out at what level (amount) in practice he ingests dairy products, both knowingly and unknowingly. But he has made a beginning on the issue, and can then decide whether or not it is worth pursuing. In this context, it is wise to remember that many of our major problems afflict us so seriously only because we ignored them early on, when they were small. On the other hand, Orientation is for clarifying your concerns and determining whether something is worth attention now: a matter of priorities.

Step 2 Why is This Difficult to Think About?

Distinguish: WHAT KIND OF DIFFICULTY DO I FEEL?
Distinguish: Is it about information or about process?
Look in/out: Should I look into the problem or outside it or at myself?
Commit: How far is it my problem? When could others help?

First of all, if you feel no inner difficulty, then of course you get on with it, confident you are not underestimating the problem. Otherwise, we should always bear in mind that what makes many a problem difficult is our perception of it.

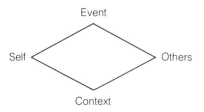

5.3 Where is the Heart of the Fire?

Somewhere in this field above created by the relationship between an event, its context, self and others, is the inner nub of the problem, the heart of the fire, the source of the personal difficulty you feel. It will be no use focusing on the event observed if what really matters is its background or context. It will be no use changing oneself, if really it is other people who constitute the problem. The heart of the fire could have less to do with the problem you first see than the factors or events that surround it, or that you compare with it. Although Gestalt and Systems Theory are now well known and clearly relevant here, in practice people can easily fail to challenge their assumptions about this.

For instance a company might invest significantly in a management development course. If a year later it is found that those who came are hardly changed in their behaviour at work, then there's naturally a post-mortem. Suppose one manager had run the course single-handed. He would spontaneously feel extremely guilty and vulnerable. He might only blame himself. Yet if he were a manager with bags of experience of success, he might wonder what had been wrong with the course itself, that is the event as distinct from his own contribution. Was it badly conceived, wrongly structured, the emphasis on all the wrong topics? It is even permissible to enquire whether the problem lay closest to the participants themselves. Such a query is not intended as a cop out or illegitimate excuse. In practice it can actually happen that participants taking part in an event at a particular time of the year are in a bad state. They can let themselves down drastically or fail to come up to the exceptional standards of performance that are often required in a programme of development. (The accelerated learning of some courses is usually much tougher to take than normal operational work.) Finally there is the operational environment, the context. It is more than possible that the failure to improve behaviour can be laid at its door. The so-called course was not treated as a learning programme embracing the issues of the workplace. Some of these powerful factors influencing the outcomes of training are the location, the hierarchy factors, the systems, even the individuals with a close personal relationship such as the immediate boss, a key subordinate, customer or supplier. Invisibly pervading them all is the organizational culture. All such factors should be addressed by the learning programme which surrounds the course. Yet this is rarely done. A frightening proportion of managers go to courses designed to help them improve their performance at work without either a briefing from their boss beforehand or a discussion of action arising from the course afterwards. If this extended example illustrates the wider issue of 'where does the real problem lie?' then it is worthwhile to locate the heart of the fire, the problem's centre of gravity between Event, Context, Self, and Others. It is essential to recognize at least part of the problem and to own that.

Step 3   Sort it Out

Set Level:	HAVE WE GOT THE RIGHT PROBLEM?
Look in/out:	What other aspects of the problem are there?
Categorise:	What connections or separations should be made?
Distinguish:	What aspects are fixed? What's critical?
Value:	Are there priorities?

One of the ways that people deal with huge quantities of information is to handle it in bunches. We bundle things of a similar nature together and treat them as one by giving them a label. This is very handy, but can sometimes be too vague and sloppy, failing to discriminate between things that only appear to be similar. When we connect the wrong things together in our minds, it can easily lead to our seizing the wrong problem or the wrong part of it. What is needed is to identify the problem in such a way as will lead directly to the most useful action to be taken.

If you find yourself asking 'What is the real problem?', it is likely things are complex. It is also likely that it will have to be broken up into parts, or it may be that there are so many parts already that a pattern doesn't naturally emerge as making any sense. In the former case, a problem that is too big cannot be digested in one gulp, and must be unravelled so as to make a start. In the latter case, you cannot focus attention properly on several different aspects at once, else your dealing with one aspect is messed up by distraction from another. Further, if you have any chance of help from colleagues, then it is good to draw useful boundaries around each sub-problem, so that it can be handed to someone who can 'own' that sub-problem or aspect of the whole. Delegation then has less consequences. 'Analyse the problem' is great advice as soon as you have defined what it is, but if we were clear about that we would not need this step of sorting it out, and could just get on with whatever type of analysis is likely to prove most useful. The point of orientation is to identify just that, how to choose the best thinking plan. So we need questions that suit any problem that is obscure.

A simple way to expose the different levels and specific parts of a problem is to pursue two fundamental questions, 'Only?' and 'All?' Starting with the first, you ask 'Only the so and so? What else?', pursuing upwards to higher levels with the question, 'What do these have in common?', that is, do they belong to a higher category? I once did this to the task facing me which I first expressed as 'Improve the lawn'. This is what it led me into:

1 *Q* Only the lawn? What else in the same category needs improvement?
  A I mean the flower-beds, trees, hedges, shrubs, but not paths, fences or gates.
2 *Q* What on a higher level are these a part of?
  A The garden of course.
3 *Q* Do I still want to improve the lawn, or something else about the garden?
  A Er . . . well . . .
4 *Q* Only the garden? What else is in the same category?
  A The outbuildings, sheds, stables, summer-house perhaps.
5 *Q* What else on a higher level are these a part of?
  A The property, our home, life savings, investment, etc.
6 *Q* Is it still the garden, or is there something else about the property that you want to improve?
  A Well, perhaps I should see to the roof first . . .

I know of no better way to avoid working on the lawn! But seriously, one should make a conscious choice of level here. The issue could usefully be explored 'downwards', or in the opposite direction. One can ask, 'All the so and so? No exceptions?', pursuing this downwards with 'Everywhere? All the time? Totally?' until the real issue is very specific. This is how it went:

1 *Q* All the lawn(s)? What different categories are there of 'lawn'?
  A The big back lawn, the front lawn, the grass paths between beds, the banks.
2 *Q* Which part concerns you most?
  A The big lawn, but not its banks, or the grass paths.
3 *Q* Is it all over? Everywhere? Where especially?
  A Bare patches, weeds, moss, but not the bumps and hollows.
4 *Q* Is it all the time, for ever, immediately?
  A No, this spring, perhaps in three stages, but not too late in case of a dry summer.
5 *Q* Should it be to absolute standards? At all costs?
  A Not likely, just as good as Mr Jones next door . . .

Specifying, of course, involves recognizing what you do not want, or what the problem might be expected to be but it isn't quite that.

The most frequent pitfall in the recognition of a problem has to do with level. Here is another approach to dealing with this everyday difficulty. Following General Systems Theory, one can instantly access a useful triad of aspects that seem to apply to most things:

STRUCTURE   Of what is this a part?
QUALITY   Of what is this a kind?
TIME-PLAN   Of what is this a stage?

First of all, structure. Practically everything is a part of something bigger. Even a large organization like IBM is still only a part of the computer industry as a whole, even Shell is only one of the Seven Sisters. We should give ourselves the conscious opportunity to determine whether to treat our problem at the level we first thought of, or at another, which must also be identified. So IBM is not only part of the computer industry but also a part of the information industry and the communications industry etc., etc. It might be critical which one we choose, if we escalate our problem to the higher level. It is obvious that the same applies to the other two aspects of the triad. Second, quality. Everything is a kind of something. Hong Kong is a kind of economic miracle, different from say that of Germany or Japan or Korea or Taiwan. To say so is to not say that it is a kind of island, which would invite quite different contexts and comparisons. Finally time-plan. Perestroika is probably a stage of some longer plan. It matters a great deal whether you see it as the evolutionary unrolling of the revolution, or whether you see it as the desperate pragmatism of a failed economy. And again whether you decide to deal with the longer plan, or the stage of it that now offers an immediate business opportunity.

We can take those three factors of structure, quality and time-plan a good deal further. They can form the basis for a kind of trinity of hierarchies, of parts, kinds and stages, each operating on three levels. We have seen that anything you consider will be a part of something greater. But also there are usually other parts of that greater thing, and further, your original object/subject has its own parts. Switzerland is part of Europe; Holland, France and Greece are some of the other parts; and Switzerland has its own cantons. Thus there is a family of grandfather, fathers and uncles, and sons (who are also grandsons). This generic hierarchy applies also to the other two members of the trinity, kinds and stages. So a Fokker is a kind of aeroplane; other kinds include Boeing and Airbus; and there are several kinds of Fokker. The event you must deal with tomorrow is probably just one stage of a longer series; there are parallel phases, as in network analysis, and your event will itself have its own stages.

Here are nine possible ways to miss or to grasp hold of the nub of your problem. Separating any situation into such compartments makes it easier to seek, recognize and judge the information about it. This trinity has enough facets to make some model of it potentially useful, and it may be significant that it is more difficult to make one that is entirely self-explanatory than you might have thought. I have struggled with the trinity for years to try and get it modelled. One option is to build a triangle whose three sides are named Time, Structure and Quality, and for each factor make a simple family tree. Pictures can make thoughts easier to remember and use. Floundering in the midst of a problem, wandering aimlessly around the outside of it, failing to communicate or understand what is being thought or said, these can all be caused by not making use of this trinity.

Moving on to Categorise, sorting out all the various aspects of any problem is not just a matter of separation. It can be as important to join together parts of the problem that at first seemed separate. Sometimes it is difficult to do this without falling prey to a vicious circle, but it must be done for one's thinking to be effective. The medical profession is often plagued by the difficulty. A conscientious doctor may actually separate out all the elements of his patient's symptoms and surrounding conditions. For example suppose the man is suffering back pain. On investigation, he separates out several items: a severe fall in October, advancing age, worry about his daughter, stress from overwork, habitual posture, diet (which itself splits into food and drink respectively) and an old injury. How can he tell which of these separate elements should more usefully be joined together? Such sorting out is key to his diagnosis and prescription. When trying to write an expert system for the medical practitioner, the difficulty attached to this aspect of sorting things out has become apparent. The computer still needs an experienced doctor to interpret and make best use of it with the patient.

Of comparable importance is the notion that some aspects of a situation facing us are fixed and others variable. We have discretion only on the variables of course. In physical matters, this is certainly true. A lever without a fixed fulcrum cannot work. Scissors missing their pivot pin are useless and so on. It is also true in problem-solving, the difficulty being to determine which parts of your problem are fixed and which variable. Often we leap unconsciously to the wrong assumptions about this, assumptions that could even have been the source of our difficulty in knowing how to proceed in the first place. When Mahomet realized the mountain would not come to him . . .

A primary tactic in thinking is to challenge and test the validity of what we have taken as read. Were we right to do so? An obvious example is supply and demand, or production and sales. How was Boeing to know which to treat as fixed and which to focus their energies on? What had been a glut of commercial aeroplanes suddenly became a serious backlog of orders owing to a massive surge in sales. Six hundred orders just in the first half of 1989 means that some orders will not be delivered for ten years. Now should they treat those orders as fixed and concentrate on how to meet them, or should they treat production capability of a proper quality as fixed and the marketing end as a variable to do something about?

The plastic bag affords an example of a different kind. What might still be seen as a question of 'How to provide cheap throw-away carriers for our goods?' is for some the question 'What can we do with billions of throw-away bags?' The first case fixes on the need for such convenient objects and the variables are various ways of making them cheaply and making gains from advertising. The second sees the bags as all too fixed and universal, the variables being how to get rid of undisposable plastic. Pursuing this a little, if undisposability is treated as fixed, then we might consider how to reduce the numbers made or how to find even further ways to exploit their indestructibility. (Worn motor-car tyres are now usefully dumped in the sea off Florida to form the basis for underwater reefs and sea life.) Or if we refuse to accept that anything should be undisposable and focus on something like ecological safety as fixed, then we look for ways to make bags biodegradable.

As a last example, we all live in a world full of causes and effects, multi-dimensional hierarchies of them. More confusing still, each cause of each effect is itself an effect of an earlier cause, and of course each effect will cause further effects. In other words, every phenomenon we can experience is at once both a cause of something and an effect of something else. Small wonder that this makes it difficult to feel confident about one's grasp on the world. Yet to grasp the world successfully, it is essential to fix one's focus. When the issue of nuclear waste comes up, it matters whether you see it as an effect of nuclear power stations or as the cause of eternal danger. Fix it as an effect, and it must then compete in your mind with the effects of other ways of producing electricity, which could be even more terrible. You could be steered away from thinking how to reduce the probability of a power station producing such noxious stuff at all. But fix it as a cause, and you are into the problems of dealing with it, how to store it safely and where; how to reassure the public, honestly; and of course into containing the seriousness in case it should ever leak out.

This is not to say that one should deal with only part of any problem. Of course not. But experience shows that nobody can look all ways at once; you cannot dither, or randomly snatch at different directions to point in. It is being unsure of direction that is at the base of any feeling of helplessness and frustration.

On setting priorities everyone knows that 'a problem defined is half-solved already'. No wonder, for definition involves so much. It demands that you are willing to ignore or discard aspects that are not the problem, or at least that cannot offer you a fairly clean, strong grip on it. This is half the secret: to find even a small part of the problem that offers a chance to pick it up and deal with it when as a whole it is too big. The other half of the secret is to choose which handhold to grab first.

I have a map for Setting Priority, which can be seen as a subroutine to be inserted inside many maps as well as this one. It is in essence a very limited form of the decision process. As it will be shown in the next chapter, I have dispensed with it here. Having identified core issues, all you want now is to decide which should be treated first, which later. Some things if not done early should not be done at all. The value of an action often depends on its timing. You may want to do the things that matter first, or only those. Unless you give full attention to core issues one at a time you will soon be back again to re-Orientation! This said, priorities reflect the subjective judgement, at the moment, of the person who sets them. So do it quickly, rather than waste time agonizing over it.

Step 4   If Only...

Pretend: WE WOULD BE UNSTUCK IF ONLY . . . .
Pretend: If only I could feel confident about what is known
                    (reaches towards → red Describe)
Pretend: If only I could come up with a new idea
                    (reaches towards → green Realise)

Pretend: If only I could resolve the struggle between my own values
            (reaches towards → blue Judge)

Where are you now? From Step 3, Sort it out, you have found what needs attention first. That was the external, you might say the objective, problem. You know what the issue is you have to tackle. You have done the complex bit. Step 4 can be got through typically very quickly. It asks: to solve the problem do you need to get more information, look for more ideas or make a judgement? If you can identify which of these needs is uppermost, you will unlock the inner mental scramble and point yourself towards the working map that you really should be using. (The Orientation map does not solve your problem. It leads you only towards identifying the way you will set about solving it.)

Let's take the example of a weekend visit to the Cotswolds. Friday morning, and I am saying 'Where the hell am I?' I am feeling rushed and muddled about what to pack and I am dithering about in clear need of orientation. My wife brings me a coffee and we stop and talk.

'What's up?' she says. I reply, 'I want to be away by 11 o'clock but I am not sure we will make it.' (Step 1.)

'Can I help?' she says. 'Well, no,' I say. 'The problem seems more to do with my sorting out what I should be doing when I get there so that I know what I must do before we leave.' (Step 2.)

My dear wife responds, 'Are you sure that's all it is?' 'Yes, but it doesn't feel that simple at the moment,' I reply truculently. 'Well, come on then, let's sort it out,' she insists. Now we are well into Step 3.

'What have you absolutely got to do when you are down there?' she asks. I list three things. 'Is there anything else? What would you like to do as well?' she smiles hopefully, since I know she wants time to see friends. I hastily revise my 'musts' and include a visit to Sarah and Ruanna as well.

'Right, so now we know what we absolutely have to do. Why is this a problem?' she asks. 'Is anything clashing, or what?'

'Well, honestly I am not sure whether to make some phone calls now to ensure people know when I shall see them definitely, or whether to leave it loose and hope it will all pan out. If I don't make the phone calls now I might not get to see everyone, but if I do we may well not get away by 11 o'clock and then that throws out my chances of getting to the jeweller in Cirencester by one o'clock – and I know he won't be there after half past one.'

So Step 3 has taken us to the nub of the problem.

'Well, can we get round this?' she says. 'Do we need more information? Is there another possibility you haven't considered? Or have you just got to make up your mind that you'll get away by 11 o'clock come what may and let fate sort out the rest of the weekend?' Yes, we have reached Step 4, and now it looks easy. But Sue may be better at this than I am.

The Thunk Pretend invites you to adopt a playful approach: We will be unstuck IF ONLY . . . Three possible scenarios are offered for exploration with the three Super-Thunks. In all three cases you are using the imagination of Pretend to envision, play the wishing game, to go beyond reality in order to reach it in a new form.

You must ask yourself which of these three 'if only's you would choose. The first is asking you whether you wish that the facts were more accurate or truthful, if you had more of them, or that the information were better organized or clearer. The second asks whether you feel the only way forward is from some completely new angle, some intuitive leap, some surprising idea. The third asks if you wish you knew what really matters to you, the relative strength of your own competing values and constraints in the light of your goal. The first is about truth, the second about imagination and the third about will.

How do the answers to these questions help you? If you can pin down inside yourself what the most important need is, you have clarified the mental energy most needed from you to resolve it. This is the reciprocal nature of the outside and insidedness of problems. Out there is also from inside here. Thunks are the intention you have from inside yourself, the activity of thinking *and* the thinking goal you want to reach outside yourself. For every situation there are effective and ineffective ways of dealing with it. Simply, when you have recognized that a situation needs imagination, don't make a hash of it by putting your values up-front. When you have seen that it requires judgement, don't go wild with wonderful ideas. When it requires investigation, do not allow either judgement or imagination to spoil the purity of the truth you need. It should always be possible to recognize different kinds of situation in terms of whether their primary need is for truth, imagination or judgement.

This 'If only' part of orientation helps you both to recognize the kind of problem you have focused on and ensure that you tackle it with the most effective kind of thinking energy. When one's mental energy is in tune with the task, you operate at your peak of performance. You bring the right tools from your mental tool-case, and everything seems easy. 'If only' you choose the approach the problem needs, the problem will be virtually over.

What was needed for the Cirencester problem? First a challenge to my assumption that I could only see the jeweller on the Friday before 1.30. This was a new idea. Maybe he would be available on Saturday or Sunday. With one phone call I could check this out. The whole picture might then take on a different shape and I would be either back into Orientation once more or on to Make a Plan. In this case, at Step 4 my problem was clarified for action and I could abandon Orientation to take action.

Step 5   Work it Out

Compare:	WHAT APPROACH WILL MATCH THE PROBLEM NOW?
Distinguish:	Which map is ready made and suitable?
Categorise:	Organise all the aspects of the process
Code:	Make a map that suits yourself

Between Steps 3 and 4, switching back and forth, you get to understand what the problem really is. The panic muddle of 'Where the hell am I?' should have subsided because you will have a sense now of whether you will need to look for ideas, information or judgement (Step 4) and in what context (Step 3). Now you know what the hell it is that churned you up, you are ready to make a plan for thinking about it in order to take action on it. You might have a simple plan for tackling it which you draw from your memory and can jot down 'on the back of an envelope'. The problem may require a more complex kind of blueprint. Whatever you use it will govern your actions until the problem is resolved or until you need to re-orientate and change it, which of course frequently happens.

Since you are seeking to identify the approach that will match the problem as you now see it you may well have met this type of problem before and can attack it by using a familiar and favoured thinking plan. For instance, you are constantly dealing with possible risks, so you have a good routine worked out for that. Perhaps you often handle design specifications, so you know the tricks of the trade for dealing with criteria. It is always to be hoped that the process of

Orientation will lead you to a ready-made map in your own repertoire that suits. Much of my work is geared to teaching managers maps that are well tried and tested so that they can access them easily from their own store of maps without having to build their own from scratch each time a problem is identified.

If there isn't a map that suits, either because the situation is really a first ever, and remains intransigent, or just because the map it requires is not known to you, then you have to make your own. Of course this is being done all round the world every hour of the day. People just naturally assemble what tools and components they have in their minds, sort out some kind of sequence, and go for it. If their tools and thinking components are haphazard, they simply appear to be muddled thinkers. If they cannot recognize what the problem needs in terms of what they have in their heads, they cannot aim their thinking, nor control and steer it when not appropriate. Jenny Lee's famous remark in the House of Commons is very apt here. 'How can I know what I think until I have said it?' Knowledge of maps and indeed your own scheme of maps helps to overcome this problem of not knowing what is in one's own head. Confidence in picking an appropriate map to suit the need enables one to hold back one's initial impulses, to plan how the problem should be addressed, and then to check whether that is the right approach, or at least roughly in the right direction. It turns you from impulsive end-gaining to considered means-whereby.

Things are now falling into place. There is a map or plan to guide one's thinking. Isn't it time to get started?

Step 6   The Map We'll Use: Commitment

Commit:	IS THIS THE WAY TO GO? DOES THE PROCESS SUIT?
Commit:	Are we (all) committed?
Test:	How and when will we take stock of progress?
Do:	Where on our map shall we start?

Orientation of some kind is being done so often at a personal and individual level so, when someone is just on their own, this last stage is not needed. Whenever others are involved it is clearly important they are all singing the same tune. The least that can be done is some form of briefing. This is well recognized, but usually dealt with either by thick background papers which are poorly accessed before the meeting, or else by a too-long rigmarole known as 'filling you in with the details before we start'. We have probably all suffered from this well-meaning effort and probably inflicted it on other people. In practice, it saves a lot of time if such a briefing is led either by skilful questions from the group, or by the problem-owner using the divers parts of the map he is working with to hang his data on. A map makes thought coherent very quickly especially if it is mapped out with a few key words on to a flip chart.

A map doesn't tell you where to start and what route to take through it. If this has already been determined by the individual on his own then all the more reason for getting agreement to his plan with others. From experience it is wise to assume that things won't work out according to plan, and therefore the question should be raised, 'How and when will we take stock again?' and go back to Orientation.

Now it is time to get started. The only purpose of all this thinking was to take action, better action than without it. At any point in Orientation, as soon as you know what to do, drop it and get on with it. Just as the moment you get lost or stuck again, pick it up.

Orientation can be complex and difficult, but in this it only matches the kinds of situation you would use it for. Far more often it is done in a matter of minutes, sometimes even seconds. It is the principles that matter, not the scope for detail and complexity. By playing a slow-motion camera on some of the issues the map deals with, I could have made it appear like an invitation to paralysis by analysis. Nothing is further from reality. Everyone knows that when you have defined the problem it is half-solved. This map is to make sure that the problem you solve is the real one, and to give the confidence to get going. Because it is a map, you have random access to it from your memory. Masterful use of this map, the most central and often used and the gateway to all others, is the hallmark of the really skilful problem-solver, the conceptual manager.

6

Build Your Own Maps

The years early on in my career as a salesman made me an enthusiast for maps. It matters so much to salesmen, because their commission depends on it, that every time they have a personal encounter whether by telephone or in person, they reflect on it and learn from it. Selling is the one operation in a business where great attention is paid to encouraging people to review what they have just done. A good field sales manager will frequently accompany his people and chew the fat afterwards. They are actually conceptualizing the event, but don't let a salesman hear you say it! The training for a sales job makes people very conscious of the way they are handling things, through teaching stratagems and plans for dealing with each kind of customer and occasion. I recall the thorough training I was given in selling routines for home calls when I worked for Hoover, and how we were encouraged to use them as the backbone of a successful call. Because we were also servicing machines as well as selling new ones we had technical routines to follow too. The Hoover training built a kind of expert system of maps and routines in my head. This system had been grown from years of other people's sales and servicing experience distilled into best practice. I count my success in selling washing machines and Hoovers to the way I then extended the maps I had been given. Soon I had my own field force and in turn tried to pass on to them the excitement and benefits of really making use of maps. Once I had learned the habit of mapping to get good results in selling I could see its application in all fields of business. I aim to show how to build an expert system for making use of expert systems of all kinds.

If you set out deliberately to build your own system of conceptual maps you would be facing what we faced at the start of the Philips project. What is different, if you care to take advantage of it, is that the Philips project and my subsequent work has provided design tools to do the job. We had to find the basic concepts first. Now they exist it is easier for others. to work out their own maps. Anyone can build their own maps successfully. You do not have to start from the bottom but can begin several rungs up. The Thunks will be your basic tools, since this is just what they were designed for: tools to make tools.

The chief advantages of building your own are that your ownership of them is stronger so your use of them will be more effective. As a salesman years ago, I found that if I 'improved' a map I had been taught to use I felt increased enthusiasm to work with it and check its usefulness for getting sales. In this way I learned more about myself, more about the variety and sameness of the kinds of task I was doing, and more about how I was thinking as I did them. Building up my own maps raised my standards of thinking, because I had to look carefully at what thinking processes I was using and whether they were satisfactory. Subsequently the quality of how I thought and the results I got were raised.

In the Philips project, we also found this improvement even while doing the original work. The benefits continue because we continue to extend our taxonomy, improve it, learn from it, in a continuing iterative spiral of development. The motto we adopted at the start of the Philips project was 'We eat our own bread'. It is a Dutch phrase, meaning in our case that everything we discovered we would use directly to develop the work further. Then, if we lived by what we learned we would surely know whether it was of any use. Everything that is described here is a reflection of what we did to build our maps originally, and what I still use in work with client organizations, sometimes very overtly and sometimes invisibly.

How far it is possible for someone to develop their own system for planning their thinking and then to use it depends on the individual, both their ability and their willingness to do so. Some people will scarcely believe it possible, and others might not even feel it desirable, especially those who believe strongly in their spontaneity. In practice we find that consultants, rather than managers, make their own conceptual tools. Consultants are professional generalists who really appreciate the value of good thinking tools, because they depend on them to cope with the variety of work they handle. Unless they are specialist experts, some of the best consultants are Jacks of all trades and masters of one – conceptual toolmaking. This enables them to operate effectively with all businesses because they have the generic tools to handle all kinds of data. Since managers will have to operate more like consultants in the coming decade, they will have to select and develop good conceptual tools too. This is far from implying that consultants are better than the managers they are assisting. It is just that the consultant has had to focus on conceptual tools in order to operate with the agility required when dealing with unfamiliar operations. The consequences of having no such way to control one's thinking process are so severe that many managers will recognize this skill as a sign of their own advancing development and maturity. It goes without saying that one cannot monitor and change the course of one's thought unless some plan or course exists in the first place.

How could the ever-changing holographic carpet of business be mapped so that thinking could be planned and monitored? Surely it's hard enough to arrive at a reasonable account of history that has already happened, never mind to chart the organic interactions of thinking processes dealing with the here and now and the unknowable future? I am confident that it can be done well enough to make it effective for the practical needs of managing. The maps already in our taxonomy, developed over many years, do work when people use them. Confidence in them grows with each passing year, as more managers work with them and find them not only valid but vital in real-time business. Time refines and develops all the maps. If a new need arises for which there isn't a map then we make a new one. Before launching into the process of map building, maps need to be set in a context, in a taxonomy of tools.

Taxonomy of Tools

Apart from a collection of major maps, some of which are described in this book, I have developed a whole range of different thinking instruments for different purposes. They are united by the common language of colours and Thunks. All are made of Thunks. They fall loosely into two types, namely task-tools and people-tools, with a third type of another order, physical conceptual tools. Because they are all made of Thunks there are cross overs between them.

The people-tools are instruments that help people understand themselves and other people as opposed to helping them directly to tackle work. Of course, by understanding themselves they are likely to perform better too, but that is not guaranteed by using the people-tools. The single most important people-tool I use is the Thinking Intentions Profile (TIP) mentioned earlier. TIP is constructed from Thunks and provides explicit awareness of one's preference for dealing with the various aspects of all the tasks faced in work and life.

The task-tools can be seen on several levels. When we first started to make these task-tools in the Philips project we saw them as temporary transfer mechanisms and hoped that as managers worked with them the physical form could be dropped as soon as the format was embedded in their minds. I thought memory would be more efficient and effective than pieces of card, especially in meetings. I wanted the conceptual processes embodied in the tools to be absorbed into the bloodstream. This did happen in part. But some tools, for instance detailed checklists, always needed to be physically consulted because the memory plays tricks. However, I have now revised my view on getting managers to memorize the tools. The activity of actually getting a tool out and looking at it breaks mental rigidities, stimulates new thinking and triggers a wider variety of thoughts. I encourage myself and others to make their thinking processes visible in physical tools as often as possible and to refer repeatedly to them not only at their own desks but most especially in meetings. Getting the tools out on the table also encourages managers to use them as prototypes rather than finished products. They are much more likely to change and adapt what they constantly look at in the flesh. After all the tools weren't meant to be perfect – we wanted the Philips managers to make their own tools using our originals as starters.

Task-Tools

Structuring and questioning tools:
> Models
> Maps
> Subroutines
> Colour-frame

Questioning tools:
> Creative instruments
> Conceptual checklists

All the tools have physical embodiments but some formats are designed to encourage a greater interaction between the user and the tool than others. I have found that the best way to hook managers on to conceptual thinking is to get them to interact bodily with the tools in a variety of formats. Just looking at maps or models is not sufficient to really learn how to use them. So all task-tools are also turned into worksheets and instruments which managers can get hold of, write on, draw on, colour, tear up, and redraw. In fact both task- and people-tools are formed into special physical tools for self questioning or group questioning, with spaces for people to write in. The TIP profile for instance is a self-administered questionnaire with a picture profile that requires you draw it up in colours. The maps are also structured as large worksheets which can be blown up to any size so that whole groups can use them simultaneously. Large-scale versions can be tabled or stuck on the wall. Particular parts can be adapted and worked with on flip charts all around the walls. A whole room then becomes a conceptual framework, a massive machine for thinking in.

With interactive physical tools like this, managers literally *feel* how their minds work as they co-ordinate their hands and eyes, kinesthetically making connections between the invisible inner thought and the visible outer marks on paper. These specially designed tools mix together physical and cerebral activity. The physical discipline improves both the quantity and the quality of thinking output. When I run my real-time problem-solving work-shops I make extensive use of many physical tools, especially Visual Gathering, which is briefly described in Chapter 3. The room becomes an outward picture of the minds of the people working together. The added benefit of physical tools is that they make you move around. This keeps the body and breathing mobile, ensuring that 'sitting-itis' doesn't deaden conceptual thinking.

What Routines are Already Used?

All of our experiences can be treated as if they were journeys, requiring maps and plans. We can view the whole of life as a complex series of overlapping plans, each consisting of stages or phases which themselves require mini-plans. Because all phases overlap and blend in with the welter of other phases of plans, it is often unclear to the individual just which plan he is currently on. Watching and participating in many managers' meetings I see that finding the process to work with crucially sets the path for the meeting. Very often to find the route they must take absorbs most of the time. In fact they are failing to orientate themselves and taking much longer than is really necessary to identify what phase of what plan they should be on.

Man's constant habit of forming new directions will sometimes compound the confusion by leaving old plans in place even though the new goals have rendered them obsolete. If Rome is on your route from London to Cairo, it may become irrelevant when you decide to go to Berlin instead. Of course we know this because there is a rough map of Europe in our heads. Which conceptual map to use for a real-time management problem is not so easily recognizable because, as our investigations showed, managers do not have an atlas of conceptual maps in their heads.

Managers are using their own conceptual routines all the time to help them with their real-time problem-solving. These are collections of aphorisms, checklists, homilies, parables, professional guidelines, maxims, proverbs, company procedures and manners, held in the memory. They represent their sets of guiding principles to help them think instantly of what to do and say. People say and write things because they are following a collection of routines from their memories which tells them 'This situation requires x or y or z from my kit-bag of experience.' As they come up against different problems they refer to one or other of their strings or clusters of thought reflexes. Theirs is not a system of maps, because these strings may be logically inconsistent with each other, but a random collection which the individual has found useful over the years. They are all idiosyncratic, personal and sometimes difficult to identify because they are operated so unconsciously.

I have looked at dozens of examples in use by managers in the programmes I have run. Some have formed the bulk of their routines quite deliberately by selecting and committing to memory those significant lessons learned from their parents, their headmaster or favourite teacher at school, from their tutor in college, their bosses, colleagues, from company trainers, even from books. But much of what runs the process of people's thinking was learned without conscious review or revision, so it is actually quite unconscious, although very active in shaping how they go about their thinking every day.

Each individual amalgamates his life experience into his own set of rules or questions which he pigeon-holes in his mind for ease of access. Methods of mental pigeon-holing are as varied as people, whose awareness of their methods is usually very low, in fact in such deep shadow that the light of consciousness is seldom invited to penetrate. But now more are beginning to look, without prompting from a consultant like myself, at some of the routines they are working with. They are beginning to appreciate how significant mental routines are in affecting business results. They can see that so many of the delays and difficulties between people arise from ignorance of one another's mental positioning or from operating with poor quality routines. In contrast, experience has shown me that good management maps, consciously used, raise standards and performance.

In the physical world people are much more aware of the power and value of maps and models. If you were lost on a moor or woodland without some official map to guide you, you would make use of the best crisis map you had in your head to find your way home; either a rough memory of the map you looked at before leaving or more likely by orientating yourself to the sun using the schematic compass you carry in your head. Crude but better than nothing. The compass model in your head is so simple that you can remember and use it in a crisis. It is truly generic at a high level. You might even manage to rescue yourself without the detail of a good map because the points of the compass are so fundamentally sound.

The highest level I have reached in all this conceptual work is embraced in the idea of a model. This is not a map at all. Ideally, I strive to reach some form of structure or dynamic relationship which epitomizes the task process through extreme simplicity. It is like looking for the elegant equation that sums the whole thing up, only that the form I seek is a spatial one, even something that can be physically made, like a real model. I have managed to get somewhere near this sublime goal for only a few models, one of which is decision-making. I have not shown it in this book as it is already publised in *The Colours of your Mind* (Fontana, 1989). A model is the ultimate. Literally so, it is the very last thing one reaches in map-building; but when you succeed in capturing the essential soul of a task it is like having designed a logo for your company which says everything about it in one symbolic form: rare and truly wonderful. The example I offer later in this book is in the work-in-progress state of a learning model, but it will serve to illustrate what is meant by the struggle for elegant truth. (See Figure 8.5.)

Rules for Forming a Map

Having shown you a map in detail in the previous chapter I now want to lead you through the process of making one for yourself.

Map as System

A map has the nature of a system, consisting only of those elements in the thought process which are proven to be essential to the satisfactory handling of the kind of situation it deals with. All elements of the system are 'musts'. They are mutually dependent and likely to operate both as stimuli to and as checks on one another.

In the selling map, for example, the step called Close prompts you to ask the prospective customer to buy. (See Figure 6.1.) If you do this at an unreasonably early stage, you should expect resistance and at least one objection. You must therefore be ready to leap to another step on the map, Be Responsive to Objections. You have to be ready with a suitable response, or think up something with agility. By playing these two steps in dynamic tension you achieve what you hope for – to discover how 'warm' your customer is and whether he is getting warmer or not. If your responses to his objections are valid for him you will accomplish the Close step all the sooner.

Generic Maps

A map should be generic and therefore as far as possible free of data. This means that all the elements and parts of the system will be applicable to any relevant situation without changing the words used in the questions. At first sight this may seem ridiculous. How can anyone think without real live data in front of him? There are two points here.

First there are questions to be asked where absolutely no knowledge is required before raising them. For instance, in a negotiation, one can say, 'Is there anything you might expect me to know already which therefore you have not told me?' This is a strong and penetrating question that can be asked and one clearly need not know anything about the particular situation to do so.

Second, it is always possible to adopt a generalized question and clothe it with information related to what's going on, customizing it to

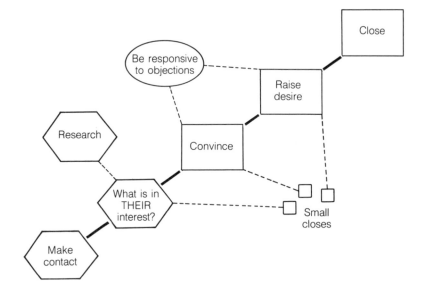

6.1 Selling Map

the event. Since I have worked with over 1,000 scientists who are engaged in advanced technological research someone working with me might be forgiven for thinking I have up-to-date scientific expertise. I do not. I was recently collaborating with the Head of a consumer electronics research laboratory. To ensure that I got the necessary technical information that he might have supposed I actually already knew I said, 'Is there anything technical I need in this project which because you know I have worked with scientists for years you have not told me? Don't forget I don't actually have a scientific background.' This produced an immediate and useful response from him. Out came some physical models to illustrate the problems, and I could grasp the issue at another level of detail. Of course because my question was clothed with data some other information was excluded from the scope of the question. The real art is to make a generic question user-friendly while remaining generic.

Six Main Steps

There should be not more than six main steps in a map, because most people cannot remember more than six items in a single grouping.

The map also needs to be laid out in a distinctive pattern, to help the memory. In a strict conceptual sense it is not really essential for a map to have a distinctive pattern, and anyway there are limits to what can be done to lay out just six items on a page such that their positions are significant. We have found however that the pattern is really important not only in helping people to remember the map but also to work with it inside their heads. They can locate it spatially inside their minds. You can watch their eyes move around the inwardly seen pattern they are referring to while they work through a problem using it.

In my system of mapping, the shapes code is significant. Colouring the shapes with the Thunks colour-code has a dramatic impact on memory. These colourful maps tap into the capacities of the right brain which responds to pictures and patterns, while the words inside the colours simultaneously connect to the left brain. This is an holistic approach to thinking to encourage right and left brain to work together. The added advantage of course is that the colours are not gratuitous, but they have meaning which implies richness of concepts beyond the words which the right brain is especially responsive to. Very few managers indeed turn up their noses at the idea of colouring their maps once they have seen the practical effect of doing so. Those few that do reject it are the ones who unfortunately have limited their thinking to mainstream left brain.

Steps and Levels

Each map is very simple at the level of its six steps. In turn, each step has not more than four or five more specific questions. The Orientation Map in Figure 5.2 is on two levels. The number of successive levels should be limited for practical purposes. When more than three levels seem necessary, it is usually best to make another map at the lower level. You can see this operating in the schema of maps on New Achievement in Figure 4.1.

There is nothing absolute about the number six and some earlier maps we made in the Philips project did have more steps, though we always stuck to single figures as a must. The reason is to do with mental ergonomics, which have profoundly influenced the physical design of our thinking tools. Most people can juggle up to six mental balls in the air, but every single extra one is exponentially more difficult. Practically any long list of items is better split into clusters on different levels. Then most people can handle up to a hundred. By the way, the 25 Thunks are an example of this, for each Thunk has several factors within it which multiplies what can be remembered downwards. Upwards, few people can remember the 25 as such, but it is easy to do so when you know them as belonging to one of only 3 Super-Thunks which each has two faces, hard and soft, into which the Thunks are grouped in threes or fours. (See Figure 3.1.)

Super-Thunks

All three Super-Thunks, Judgement, Information and Ideas, must be represented. Given the scale of task for which a map is used, we have found that to leave out any Super-Thunk altogether, that is one colour, is a grievous failing, although the relative strengths can vary of course. In my experience the maps and routines for thinking that people are already using miss out on the green Thunks, so their way of handling problems is impoverished and sometimes disastrously so. As I mentioned in Chapter 1, imaginative thinking needs to slip in and out of relevance, but most business cultures fail to encourage people to do this. Better maps can correct this.

While it is important to include all the colours in a map, you do not always need to include both hard and soft aspects. Sometimes it is absolutely imperative to exclude one or the other. For example in trying to find out the cause of something that has gone wrong or gone better than expected, it is essential to exclude soft blue as far as humanly possible, because it is not only irrelevant but likely to actually get in the way of good investigation. When some disaster occurs, such as the Lockerbie air crash, the Kings Cross fire or the Alaska oil tanker spillage, the natural warmth of human feelings has to be rigorously excluded from the approach of the investigating teams. This can sometimes be an insuperable challenge. This is why soft blue is positively excluded from the map of explaining a variance.

Layout Conventions

A number of layout conventions can be adopted. The most used ones are: showing time as going from left to right and downwards rather than upwards, and never from right to left; scaling type-sizes so that more important things are large and bold; forming patterns to distinguish central from peripheral concerns. Whatever is designed should somehow reflect visually the nature of the thinking process concerned.

How to Build a Map

I set about creating a map from scratch by first identifying an activity that applies to a wide range of situations that can somehow be classified together. For instance, it is possible to see selling as similar to teaching and yet significantly different. The difference would lead me to conceive a classification of activities at a higher level to include both selling and teaching and also advertising, advocacy and negotiation. I would name this Influencing People and I would hope to build a useful map to do this. The maps I have named and constructed in this way represent a network of maps which show the way I have cut life's cake. No taxonomy can claim to be absolute or complete. Mine represents a major part of my world-view of thought.

Busy managers are usually impelled to create a map because they have recognized that they need one. 'For heaven's sake that's the third time in three months that I've messed up on a negotiation. It's about time I got clear in my own mind how the hell I should be tackling it.' This is the kind of energy that will lead someone to work out a map for negotiating, or influencing people. Managers are not likely to be concerned whether the map is part of an holistic taxonomy as I am. They will grab whatever works. So it has been my mission first to encourage them to make maps whenever they need them, situationally. Second I do also encourage them to interconnect their maps so they see system-wide how they build up their patterns of problem-solving. This enables them to recognize where patterns repeat, where they can relate to other people's maps and so improve their chances of collaborating with other people's thinking. This, of course, is holism.

As soon as I have a title, like Influencing People, it becomes the thinking goal of the new map. The whole of the map is therefore devoted to raising the questions which, when the answers are found, will satisfy that goal. According to my rules for map-making I must seek out six main steps. I would try to identify them using four different methods. I will use the Influencing People map as a working example here.

My first approach would be to draw on my experience and try to answer the question 'What has to happen conceptually for someone to be influenced?' Here are some examples:

He must feel it is in his interest to be influenced.
The case you make must seem rational and likely to work.
He must have enough information about the issue.
He must feel he fully understands.
He must not feel pressured, but rather feel he owns the idea himself.
He must have been given scope to convince himself out of what he says or does or imagines.
We must have gained enough respect for the influencer.
. . . and so on.

I would take the list above and use it as my crude starting point for creating the steps of the map. Each of these steps is a sub-thinking goal within the overall goal. Such goals, when met, would surely cause anyone to be influenced? Well, they would increase the probability. They are not good enough as yet to form the main elements of a map, for they do not cover the whole field. Already there are more than six and others are indeed missing. No matter. We shall proceed empirically, finding out through usage. Conceptual elegance is a criterion for a map, and it is demanding work. It has to be based on extensive experience and a great deal of trying and trying again.

The steps in the maps must be universal. The examples above therefore are conceptual processes, data-free. To suggest 'Sit down and write a cheque' as a step would not qualify. It is merely an action that might influence some situations but not others. A more conceptual question is 'What's in it for him?'

Another route to finding the main steps, and one I often use as my starting point, is to scan the Thunks and see what they suggest. I pick out the ones that seem appropriate. For influencing the Thunk Value is an obvious choice. So somewhere in the map must be a step that ensures that the values of the person you are seeking to influence are acknowledged and responded to. Another obvious Thunk is Code. If you want to influence someone you speak their language and relate to their perspectives. Another possible Thunk is Pursue. Influencing can very often take a long time, so you will need to employ a wide variety of approaches again and again and again. At this stage, the way I am putting down my thoughts is very loose, but I am gradually building up the range of options out of which I will refine my six main steps.

A third method is to use the colour-frame introduced in Chapter 3. It is a very useful tool for making maps. Given the constant framework of the six boxes, you can ensure that you work out six steps covering all the colours in both hard and soft. This meets one of the important rules in map-making mentioned earlier.

Working with the six boxes causes me to think of some new possibilities:

The case you make must be demonstrably likely to work.	He must have enough information to understand.	Give him a chance to build his own variations.
He must feel it is in his interest to be influenced.	The way you say it must suit his style.	He needs to listen with an entirely open mind.

I hope you are already itching to jot down better ones. The colour-frame only gives a start and your experience would quickly strengthen each box with a few other points. The next step is to assign relative importance, which can be done simply by numbering the boxes 1 to 6 (1 scores high). If it is a generic map you are making beware the influence of personal thinking style here. It is entirely possible that your own style could bias the map you build. I always have to guard against putting too much emphasis on green.

In my way of mapping I only number the steps when I am using the map as a plan, that is, when I am following it for a specific situation in the here and now. Numbering the relative importance of the six boxes is a simple but powerful way to focus your mind on what really matters, and even to register things to avoid, such as soft blue values when investigating cause, as mentioned before. This might alert you to acknowledging that even in a supremely analytical process such as diagnosis, some soft blue Prediction and Interpretation is inevitable and you will ultimately have to Commit to the findings of your analysis in a report.

Just as you can carry in your head the North, South, East and West of a compass, so you can carry the boxes of the colour-frame. It thus provides the ideal tool for recognizing thinking goals and the questions needed to reach them, and then for storing the answers to those questions. It is a kind of digital model.

Finally the steps can be constructed from subroutines. As this name implies it is a coherent assembly of related components which can be treated as a self-contained module. A subroutine is a meaningful string or cluster of Thunks which as a whole makes a contribution not only to one map but also to many others as well. It is a recurring or repeatable chunk of thinking which can be treated like a thought-bucket and carried from one situation to another, more or less unchanged.

For example, in all tasks, there is a recurring need to do the following sub-tasks:

store information	list agenda	establish criteria
set priority	test levels	challenge assumptions
define	check quality	identify
generate ideas	anticipate risk	check perception
persuade	review	set goals
etc.		

The subroutines needed for any particular map can be quickly pulled out of this network of subroutines. They will not always be used as main steps in the map but they will certainly be needed somewhere, possibly at the level of one of the questions within a main step. As soon as you recognize where you will need subroutines with which you are already familiar, your map building is speeded up. Your own subroutines might be expressed as mnenomics, word plays, proverbs. These have been routinized in your mind with enough confidence to let them run without a sense of struggle or difficulty. They are ready-programmed in your mind and hence very efficient. 'This is a bit I know how to do' is the feeling. Finding a subroutine is like coming through the foggy night into an area that is well lighted: you can go faster with confidence. It is a sub-map.

Thunks are ideal for expanding the number of subroutines you have at your disposal. Configurations of related Thunks, similar, complementary, opposing or reacting, frequently create subroutines. Any kind of subroutine can be analysed to find the Thunks in it. You can improve what you already use by checking out the Thunks within them.

Thunks as Building Blocks for Subroutines

You can view each Thunk as a set of intentions with predictable outcomes. Like the pieces in chess, they move according to their own rules. Because you know how a knight can move (its rules), you can predict its scope and where it is able to jump to next. In a sense the piece and its move are one. In the same way a Thunk suits certain objectives that a person might have and it is capable of carrying out certain intentions. Thunks are tools for particular jobs. The job and the intention are one. If you wish to capture the queen or checkmate the king, you ask yourself, 'Have I got a piece that moves like this?' Or 'What can I expect out of my three pawns, a bishop and a castle? What are they able to do?' Obviously, you cannot play chess at all until you can recognize what moves pieces can make. The master skill is then to see the patterns in the developing game which reveal what will be necessary to win.

Another image of Thunks is that they are each just bristling with questions. Questions are like statements that can be made before you know their answer, whereas statements are answers to questions that might have been asked. In a way the question selects and shapes the answer to it in advance, just as the hand-tool you use shapes the result of your action with it.

Finally, the real nature of a Thunk is to be an organic building block or molecule with a structure and an energy of its own which make it want to form into strings and clusters of larger organisms. Like the characters in a play that seem to take over from the writer and develop the story themselves, so Thunks seem able to make something work partly under their own energy. Perhaps this accounts for the phenomenon we all experience of being carried along by our own thinking, not fully in control of it.

Now it should be coming clear, especially employing this organic characteristic, how you can make subroutines and maps from Thunks for any purpose you have in mind. I like to build bottom up. I pick up a likely-looking Thunk, and knowing its effects I check to see it will take me towards my goal. Some Thunks are more likely to than others. As in any physical activity, you can put your moves together, building them into a coherent subroutine, seeking others if not satisfied. You must of course have an aim in mind to steer your choices.

All the 25 Thunks have special relationships between them, so that to use one will attract either support or counterbalance from another. For instance, if you Predict or Interpret with a view to opening out towards a future possibility, either of them invites a green Challenge, 'What assumptions are you harbouring?' Challenge wants to push thinking deeper so as to enlarge the scope of the ideas, because your assumptions may be limiting your future possibilities. If you are using the same two Thunks Predict and Interpret to draw yourself towards a final conclusion and commitment to action, immediately hard blue Test strikes, 'How sound is that?' Test is a gatekeeper that tries to prevent someone reaching an unsound commitment. In different circumstances then, either Challenge or Test will cluster with Predict and Interpret. The number of combinations of 25 Thunks is, as the makers of the Rolls-Royce motor-car used to say when asked about its horsepower, adequate.

Suppose you wished to persuade a group of people over whom you had no authority to do something which they might resist. It's possible to prepare a little string of Thunks to help you like this:

Observe	Find out about what they are like
Compare	Compare their values, opinions and likely interpretations with your own
Test	Make your argument sound
Re-describe	Anticipate unexpected reactions
Code	Tune your message to their way of hearing it
Observe	Ask and tell, show and watch
Escape	Respond resourcefully
Interpret	Make things clearer
Commit	Agree together

Not good enough on its own perhaps, but it makes a start and is certainly worth a few minutes because of what will be triggered in your mind. You have a home-made subroutine on 'persuasion'.

Let's suppose your meeting with them turns out successfully. A month or two later, you have to make a presentation. At first sight you might be tempted to write down the same set of Thunks for Present as for Persuade. The two tasks probably have much in common. Then it begins to emerge that there has to be a difference in emphasis perhaps. It is these additional Thunks that appear below for Presentation:

Realise	Preparation – open out to new ideas
Categorise	Classify the information
Distinguish	Label it logically
Set Level	Be sure you deal on the right level of abstraction for the subject
Compare	Make whatever comparisons are required

Of course I have purposely made several assumptions about the two situations. Every one is different, and you would choose the Thunks for your string situationally, to suit the occasion, the audience and yourself.

As a final example of a string, I have in mind an excellent book about information storage for professionals by V. Stibic, a manager of communications in Philips and a real authority on the subject (*Personal Documentation for Professionals*, North Holland, 1980). Years ago he saw that large numbers of people with advanced know-how of one kind or another would need to design their own filing systems for their specialist work which would have to be done even at home personally and not by secretarial staff. In the days when I worked as an employed manager in a large organization, the job of filing was considered a very menial chore and delegated accordingly. As the old joke goes, 'Shall I file these papers, sir, or will you need them again?' For know-how professionals information storage and retrieval is vital to their business and development and is a high-level task. A straightforward string for storage of information might go like this:

Observe	Scan the content
Specify	Look with more penetration, especially noticing what it seems to be but actually is not
Compare	Compare it with appropriate papers/files
Distinguish	Label it logically
Code	In a way you will easily recall
Categorise	Put it in the right file

Stibic was an information-handling professional. He would not be satisfied with the list above. He says that, in practice, any classification that is strictly and perfectly logical is quite vulnerable. He would certainly pick up on Code in this connection, but he would go further and say that it is worth considering an unusual or green approach to this so obviously analytical task. That scientific conference paper on advanced topology for instance might better go under the stairs with all the stuff you have on visits to Sweden, for the conference was in Stockholm and you always associate the material with Sweden rather than its properly-kindred subjects. You probably even call it your Swedish paper.

If you were to use a string like the one above often, improving it from experience over time, you would end up with one that would be fairly robust and stable. Possibly you would also make another string for gathering information, another for the systematic purging of files, perhaps one-twelfth of all files every month, so as to throw out the useless and keep the system fresh and alive. Such strings for differing but related tasks develop some coherence as a group, which in turn becomes a subroutine on another level. By networking and grouping like this, routines establish themselves in the mind, only most people do not try to do this consciously. As a manager in GKN I started doing this consciously myself to save time and to assure the outcomes of whatever I did. I have continued to use some of the checklists I made more than twenty years ago. Even then I would reduce them in size so as to keep in my pocket-book for quick reference. Gradually they form themselves firmly even into my dreadful memory, and now I carry them in my head insted of my pocket. One I have used a thousand times was a checklist for general design purposes. It was a F-A-B-U-T-E-S-S idea.

Function	Time
Adaptiveness	Economy
Balance	Safety
Uniqueness	Simplicity

Nothing much, you might say, but it has made sure many times that some aspect that might not have been considered was not left out. Needless to say, because the list has been so frequently used in so many different situations, each single word in it is rich with associations. It sparks my thinking and gives direction and confidence and that is why for me it works. It is also why I encourage people to make their own checklists.

The other reason why such checklists work is that there is more in them than meets the eye. The items have certainly been drawn from specific actions, events and experiences, but their special strength is that they get used often and this must be, by definition, because they apply to many occasions. They are not just data-specific but generic. In every experience there is some data and some process. It is the process aspect that is portable, transferable, learnable and worth making a tool of in some way.

Only this afternoon did I recall how as a small boy in my school, St Bede's, Stafford, we were each encouraged by the remarkable headmaster, Stafford-Northcote, to keep a little notebook in which to capture anything that struck us as specially useful in helping to learn other things. It was called *Multum in Parvo*, much in a small space, and without my realizing it until this moment has undoubtedly had a lot of influence on me over the past fifty years. Key ideas and formulae, small tools, so travel light. Boil things down and use often. What amazes me now is that Multum in Parvo was not for information, facts, lists of Latin words, but for generic ideas, patterns with many uses. If every manager kept his own Multum in Parvo the level of conceptual teaching and learning between colleagues would rise exponentially.

A final example of a robust subroutine is Set Priorities, sometimes used as a map in its own right. It appears over and again in maps, not only in Orientation. Setting priority is something you always do when two or more activities compete for your attention and time. Using this subroutine regularly soon makes it less likely that one chooses the wrong thing to tackle under pressure. It is no use to say one should always do the 'big one' first. To do it may need more time than you've got and meanwhile, by ignoring something more urgent, the fuse is busy burning on something that could easily be dealt with quickly.

This simple subroutine shows how the task of setting priority separates into two: objective fact and logic on one side, and more subjective discretionary scope on the other. Confront the left side first, because it is both overriding and easy.

ABSOLUTE FACTORS objective	DISCRETIONARY FACTORS subjective
Specify Deadlines	Value How big, serious, important?
Judge Dependency due to logical necessity	Predict How quickly can I get it done?
	Predict Diminishing or worsening?
	Value Fear x might do it before me? Do I want someone else to do it?
	Escape Can I 'cheat'?

Using Maps

When someone asks for help I jump first to Orientation to identify
what kind of map is needed. If the right kind of map does not exist
then I start to make one. At first it is rough and ready, and its
relationship within the taxonomy is not clear. A rough one can be
made very quickly, and often you have to be quick because there isn't
time to cogitate for long. I start to use it immediately on the problem
in hand. Some parts of it will really work, the questions are spot on.
Other parts do not. Since with one eye I am tackling the problem,
while with the other I examine my way of tackling it, my perceptions
and learning are heightened. This double vision is the hallmark of the
conceptual manager, for he is then a learner *par excellence*. Of course
you cannot look both ways at once. The art is to move backwards and
forwards between, as it were, the figure and the ground so that the
one clarifies the other.

Building a good map can take years. I have been working on a new
learning map since 1984 and still feel unsatisfied, although I will show
where I have got to in Chapter 8. Building a lasting taxonomy is
probably never accomplished. I am finding that as the needs of the
time change so the development of new maps and their placement in
the taxonomy is in flux. This seems healthy. For instance, in the mid-
eighties business in the UK and Europe was in dire need of
enterprise and innovation. This led me to develop the taxonomy of
maps around New Achievement, as shown in Figure 4.1. What will be
required in the 1990s? The need for a good taxonomy centred around
learning?

Beware putting too many maps into your taxonomy. Keep the
numbers of your key maps to five or six so that you can remember
them all, and then use them from memory in real-time situations.
Make them part of your thinking process so that you can access them
at will. It is acceptable in some cultures, for instance among
engineers, to refer to checklists in meetings. In many other contexts
you will need the maps at your fingertips mentally, so you can operate
with them spontaneously, in the heat of the moment. Which five or six
will you be using? Well, look at the five or six maps you are using now
and then review them in the light of this chapter.

Before you build a new one always ask 'Is there an existing map
that will do the job?' One map may do many tasks which appear to

have different names. 'Cause analysis' so well developed by Kepner Tregoe, can be adapted and used not only to explain a negative variance, but to find the cause of success, for most kinds of diagnosis or fault-finding, to resolve a dispute, and to dis/prove a statement or theory. I have even adapted it so as to convince someone about a conclusion drawn, to waterproof a case, and to anticipate a future variance from a plan. A really generic map of decision makes connections, especially at the subroutine level, with many aspects of design, planning, innovation and strategy formation; with evaluation, persuasion, negotiation, selling and marketing; with investment, purchasing and resource allocation; with appraisal, recruitment and career counselling; with teaching and writing.

Possible Maps
as suggested by Thunks

Commit to a contract	Find a market niche
Make forecasts	Inter-firm comparisons
Interpret the market	Test a takeover defence document
Set goals	
Observe performance	Organise the logistics
Present the case for merger	Write product specifications
Europe or global operations?	Create a divisional budget
Challenge tax assumptions	Form the company image
Find exceptions to legislation	Sense the future
Reposition the business	Build scenarios
Pursue research	Liquidity: stay flexible

The key to this whole mapping concept is revealed in the previous paragraph in the phrase 'especially at the subroutine level'. Almost every map is usable as a subroutine for others. They are all interconnectable. It doesn't matter whether you make your own map or borrow and adapt someone else's. You can cannibalize parts of one routine and glue them in with parts of others, so long as you are true to the main object in view, the thinking goal. In principle the question of level does not alter what's just been said. The advantage is in being able to use and reuse in many, many configurations the same subassemblies and the same components. This is the dream of the mass manufacturer, to have only few infinitely flexible parts. It is the dream of all those following Schumacher who try to develop alternative and simple technology that is really practical in the Third World. It is the dream, strangely perhaps, of at least a certain kind of philosopher. And it is the answer to a certain kind of manager's prayer: flexibility, economy and simplicity. The kind of manager whose prayer we are trying to answer is the conceptual manager.

7

Quality Assurance on Thinking

Most of the time thinking seems to just happen. There is an enduring feeling that one cannot be held responsible for thoughts that enter one's head. In the British legal system, you cannot be brought to trial for thoughts you have entertained, unless or until you materialize them into physical actions, along the lines of the old children's doggerel, 'Sticks and stones may break my bones, but words will never hurt me'. (What rubbish!) Loitering with intent to steal is a borderline case, like dumb insolence when a soldier is clearly contemptuous of his sergeant-major without actually saying anything. If however you should kill someone, the thinking behind the action, your intentionality, is recognized in the quite different charges of manslaughter and murder. The Christian church has accumulated a lot of know-how over the centuries about the culpability or otherwise of thinking. Christians pray forgiveness for what they have not done as well as what they have done, for thoughts as well as words and other deeds. There is blame for inviting conditions likely to give rise to wrong behaviour, the *occasio* of sin, and for entertaining or sustaining interest in temptations and other 'bad' thoughts.

Some current thinking even seems to support the ancient notion that thoughts actually have a physical existence and are a force to be reckoned with, even over long distances and periods of time. Whatever view one has about the physical reality of thought, I certainly treat my thinking as if it were physical. This enables me to 'get hold of it' as if it had substance. I can then turn it into visible and tangible tools which enable me to subject my thinking processes to more control. I am a convinced proponent of the idea that thinking can and should be subject to control or quality assurance. The more spontaneous we want to be, the more the need for quality assurance. That may read as a paradox but actually what most people describe as spontaneous is an unfree knee-jerk reaction in the mind. Man is aware, and aware that he is aware too, but this second or higher level is, in my view, far too infrequently visited. I would sum up the efforts of most of my teaching life as being centred in stimulating and encouraging people to develop this higher level of awareness. With self-discipline, enthusiasm and practice it is possible to markedly improve one's control over the ways in which one thinks and thus the thoughts you get from your thinking. You can determine what to do with thoughts that emanate from within before they are let out to wreak possible havoc in the external world. You can quality-assure the intentions of your mind.

Three Phases of Thinking

To quality-assure any kind of problem-solving I do, whether sitting at my desk, holding a meeting or managing a project, I manage my thinking in three phases: planning, real-time observation in action and reflection.

Phase 1   Plan your Thinking

How can you plan to think without thinking? Of course you cannot, but in practice it doesn't matter, because the two are the same thing on different levels. You think up the plan of how you will think, and then you work through the plan and think the thoughts. I use maps as the basis of my thinking plans. As I make the plan, the process of my thinking becomes visible and therefore steerable. Everyone is used to making plans for action. To build a summerhouse, you plan for weather, delivery of materials, hire of plant because the consequence would be not only inconvenient and costly, but tangibly visible. But not everyone is used to making a plan for thought. For most people it is a completely new idea. People are naïvely optimistic about having the wit to avoid or overcome problems so long as they arise only in the realm of thought and not in the realm of action. I do not hold with the view that thinking sloppily or in a stupid order can be wiped out later on by better thinking, without paying a price. Poor planning of thinking has a price which might be measured sometimes even in lives lost. Planning your thinking needs to be taken seriously because the way you plan will play a large part in affecting the outcome.

The essential task in planning is to select the items to make up your plan and sequence them.

Select for quality

As a craftsman chooses the tools he will use to achieve a quality job carefully so the wise manager chooses his thinking operations. Making a table or a chair, the woodworker will select from his kit the tools he needs, a saw, a chisel, a plane, a bradawl. The 25 Thunks are my tool-kit from which I select. Will I need to get accurate detailed information? Then I should select Specify. Will I need to persuade? Then I should select a run of Thunks Observe, Code, Interpret, Value. Often just by looking at my tool-kit I am stimulated to make appropriate selections. The tools I need seem to spring out of the Hexagon in Figure 3.1 almost shouting 'You'll need me for . . . ' Naturally I also turn directly to the maps to see if there is one ready-made which will save the basic chore of picking out the tools from scratch. Maps display the Thunks tools ready sorted for different kinds of thinking jobs. It is as if, in the maps, I have pocket-sized assistants who dutifully and neatly offer the tools I need without my having to get them out myself. These assistants do the selection for me.

Select to reduce effort

Picking the right tools in advance and selecting the right map to follow takes advantage of the principle of inertia. Once a pathway has been traced into the future, it acts as a kind of watercourse, collecting any energy (water) that is around, and funnelling or channelling it along the pathway traced in planning. An image that comes to mind is the Castrol TV advertisement, 'liquid engineering' in which the oil magically runs down a predetermined path. Maps provide pathways into the future. When I overcome my natural laziness about planning my thinking, and select an appropriate map, it directs my thinking so that inertia works for me instead of against me. Using it to guide me I can concentrate my energy on producing the thoughts that it invites me to think, rather than worrying about whether I'm going in the right directions. The energy thus saved by pre-planning will sustain my effort during the hard work of thinking through the task itself.

Select for confidence

Quality is delivered by a confident craftsman. If you use an appropriate map, it raises your confidence in the quality of the process you intend to follow. You know you are aiming your thinking right so the probability of success is higher. Confidence enables effective people to undertake high risk activities with equanimity. They are not blind fools: the risks are mostly calculated ones. When the situation is beyond a certain ceiling of uncertainty, especially handling data that is completely unknown to them, all they've got is confidence in their thinking process.

Thinking tools give me the confidence to take responsibility for delivering results when I am contracted to run real-time innovation workshops. This event, compressed within a week, gathers in specialists and managers to tackle a major issue. It is endeavouring to accomplish within a three to five day time frame what would normally take months to do. The process that is structured for these people to think together fast, imaginatively and truthfully, is all important. I build, shape, steer, unform and reform, and drive this process out of Thunks and maps.

Sequencing

Sequence in planning your thought is determined by logic or by personal bias. In the world of physical reality logic dictates that a cause always comes before its effect, and when planning your thinking this is a good rule to follow – sometimes. But what is notable about the realm of mind is that it is possible to imagine an effect first and by wanting that effect to then think up possible ways to cause it. So reversing the application of the laws of logic is a useful trick in planning your thinking. Indeed this ability to switch the direction of time makes it necessary to allow thinking to enjoy variety in sequencing. So according to your confidence or your concern you can choose in what order to use your thinking.

It is also important to take account of your personal bias when planning. Our private mental energies have perhaps the greatest impact on the course of thought, so it is advisable not to put your 'worst' thinking energy first on the list. I am not a lover of hard red detail, so when working out how I shall approach a task I tend to put steps that require imagination at the beginning to warm myself up for the (to me) tough task of getting down to detail at a later stage.

To adopt a workable sequence certainly increases confidence. It gives a sense of direction. The worst feeling one can get in thinking is of being directionless, rudderless, hopelessly at sea.

Phase 2 Real-time Observation in Action

Once in the hurly-burly of action, it's difficult to think about thinking and yet essential to observe and steer when it goes off course. It is easier to do this observation if two conditions are fulfilled. The first concerns the task, and the second yourself and other people. First the task. If you have already made a thinking plan (Phase 1) then you have a means or checking off where you have got to as you go along. It might be jotted on scrap paper, or you may be carrying it in your head. No matter, it is your guide. You also need awareness of whether you have really done the thinking that the plan asked you to do. It's no good looking at your plan, seeing it tells you to Test after you have Compared, and disobeying it – unless you disobey quite consciously through choice rather than laziness or sloppiness. The Thunks offer this unique advantage of labelling the task in the same terms as the thinking energies of your mind, so there is no excuse for not supplying the right kind of thinking. Of course, you need to be fluent with the Thunks, but that comes surprisingly quickly once you start playing the game. How long does it take to learn chess, to touch type, to play Monopoly? If you keep the instruction cards with you, you can start at once. Keep the Hexagon Array in Figure 3.1 handy.

Second, yourself and other people. Thunks offer a simple way not only to observe your own thinking in action but also any other people involved. Thunks are standard components which do not change from one moment to another, from one situation to another, or from one person to another. They are immensely helpful to interpret how other people are thinking. 'By their fruits you shall know them.' People's behaviour, the words and gestures they use, reveal the Thunks they are working with. 'Aha,' I say to myself, 'she appears to be very severe with me at the moment but I can see she is really using Test, and quite rightly is pushing my thinking to operate more carefully with Distinguish and Compare.' So don't take it amiss and enjoy the rigour of tough questioning. Notice if a Thunk is not operating when it should. If, for instance, a group of colleagues has agreed to pool information then they should be using, as a minimum, a combination of Specify, Categorise and Observe. Watch to ensure that these at least are used, and check that Set Level and Look in/out, two underused Thunks, are not forgotten.

Fast initiatives and response in pressurized management jobs demand that thinking is situationally automatic. Real-time thinking using Thunks would be impossible in the split seconds available, unless you have mastered them through practice. A skilful footballer has not only rehearsed and practised for such crisis situations from all the angles he can imagine, but he also knows how to win enough space to allow him to make his own choices. In the hurly-burly of the football goalmouth, all he can go on is his instinctual reflexes. How on earth does a top-class striker control all the variables in the chaos and carnage of the goalmouth? Split second decisions are required. The ball may come sailing through the air or driven through a forest of legs inches above the ground. If it comes in high, he must work out whether to get his head to it or his body, or his boot; should he jump or wait, turn or go forward; how to elude the defender marking him; when to shoot and where to get past that octopus of a goalkeeper? Like the agile manager, he is employing a phenomenal mix of programmed and situationally conscious skills. His move in to the goalmouth is conscious, even strategic. But when the chance comes, his header will be as it were instinctive. When under such pressure, you are glad that you have rehearsed the situation before. Planning and practice enable you to recognize in a flash what is going on and what has to be done. Luckily there are only so many things that can happen and that you can do. Thunks are conceptual tools for recognizing them in terms of the thinking action required. Let's pretend the ball coming across has got 'kick me' (Specify), 'head me' (Set Level), 'trap, turn and shoot' (Re-describe) written on it. Conceptual tools like this assure the quality of performance at the gallop and inform the review and feedback after the event. This applies both to the footballer and to the manager under pressure, though a footballer like Gary Linneker is using physical as well as mental muscles and his transfer value might be a lot higher!

Phase 3   Reflection, or Control after the Event

In my days as an area manager with Hoover I well remember being rewarded for a quarter's successful selling with a visit to the washing machine factory in Merthyr Tydfil, Wales. These days I would see this as a necessity for all salesmen rather than a reward for a few, but times were different then. As a field salesman I had naturally been sensitive to the quality of our products especially because we sold machines by live demonstration. Quality in the late 1950s was looked after mainly by control at the end of the line, once the washing machine had been made. Quality control was a reject function, with very little feedback into the total system to prevent rejections in the future. The quality assurance concept of today is system-wide and ideally ensures that there are no rejects. However this is easier to achieve in the physical production of designed goods by designed processes repeated many times in the same way than for the mental production of solutions to problems never before encountered. So it is realistic to assume that everyone will sometimes deal with some difficulties rather inadequately. I know I do.

When this happens I make a point of looking back on my thinking. I can usually see where I might have gone wrong just by sitting and recalling what happened. If I want a more robust critique I need to measure my performance against a standard. The standard is the task map I used or one of my situation specific thinking plans. It shows what should have happened. Working back through a detailed map, re-examining the questions missed, the Thunks omitted or not followed through in enough depth, enables me to do two things. First, I can quality check myself. Where are my weaknesses? Mine is with some of the red Thunks, especially Categorise and Specify. This weakness shows up again and again until I take myself in hand and correct my fault by really paying attention to those parts of maps which require me to use red Thunks. Second, I can quality check my thinking plan. Maybe things went wrong because my plan was wrong, or the map I used wasn't good enough. Perhaps I did follow my plan and my confidence in it was misplaced. This leads me to examine my plan and ask myself was it as good as it could have been. Would I change it now with hindsight? Through this double review, inwards to myself and outwards to my maps and plans, I improve my standards and raise the quality assurance in my thinking for future events.

For quality control there has to be a visible means of checking the difference between the product and its measurable parameters and standards. To quality control thinking, maps and Thunks provide the visibility against standards by virtue of their being stable descriptions of thinking performance. They have been very productively used for quality control for several years now by R & D scientists in Philips. As individuals and in groups they are encouraged to make flow charts of the ways they do their scientific development. The flow charts are made of colour-coded Thunks. They use their charts as a feedback tool to improve both their methods of development and the flow chart itself. With the common language of Thunks which everyone can apply to the diverse aspects of their work in the same way, they can mutually quality assure their thinking processes.

System-wide Quality Assurance

Quality assurance in manufacturing has evolved from the rather concrete practice of quality control on the end product to the more abstract approach of improving the manufacturing process system-wide. In quality assurance nowadays, there is more simulation, more pretending to generate scenarios with the mind, more anticipation, more pre-emption of contingencies. The ratio of thinking to doing is higher in today's more advanced and sophisticated production systems. This ratio should also apply to all the work done by 'the brain of the firm' an idea developed by Bob Garratt in his book *Creating a Learning Organisation. A Guide to Leadership, Learning and Development* (Director Books, 1990). Managers must practise quality assurance on their thinking to raise the effective intelligence of the brain of the firm of which they are all a part. Of course this cannot be done by individuals in isolation. All those members of a firm who see themselves as being paid to think need to collaborate on it.

There are ways of operating jointly to quality assure the brain of the firm, in meetings, in setting up systems, in working on personal computer networks, in managing projects, in forming training programmes and so on. Chiefly what is required is that people become much more explicit in labelling and signalling what thinking processes they are using. They will have to learn to be overt about when they are at the stage of generating ideas, green Thunks, of getting more information, red Thunks, of making judgements, blue Thunks. In many organizations where the Thunks and their colours have been introduced people will readily say, 'We need some red thinking here', or 'Too soon for blue, we must stay in red.' Or 'We're stuck. This needs green.' In one firm a memo to the Managing Director asked him to recognize that what was offered in the memo were thoughts in green, implying that they should not be treated as if they were meant to be a sound case in blue. This brought a delighted smile from the director, who had previously instituted an organization development project in order to encourage system-wide greater imagination among his actuarially inclined (blue-red) staff.

To quality assure what goes on by the brain of the firm in meetings, companies need to develop a culture where it is permissible for people to work together with plenty of paper stuck round the walls. Then structures for thinking can be drawn on to the paper in bold writing with felt pens to colour-code in red, blue and green if people know it. Each sheet becomes a thought-collecting box, labelled with the kind of thought it is expected to attract. The labels are determined by a map which everyone shares. 'So this is a decision meeting, is it? Well, the map we'll use is this one then.' Out comes the decision map, and up go the main steps of the map on to the wall, with leading questions from the map heading each thought-collecting box. As and when the people in the meeting have their thoughts they discuss them, write them on chits and stick them into the appropriate box. As the issues develop people constantly get up and down, pointing to the chits they want to discuss further, coaxing a colleague to come over to discuss an idea mounted in another part of the room. Some people hardly sit down at all. You can imagine the kinds of interchange. Chits are torn down and resurface in a new location. Some are rewritten many times. They are clustered and overlapped as the same ideas are recognized and crop up in different contexts. Unlikely bedmates are connected. Such an event is a major departure from the deadening lumpen sag that most people fall into when they sit for any length of time in a meeting. As they sink into their chairs their energy droops and their minds too, collapsing into rigid and unimaginative thinking patterns. In an active meeting such as I have described the lazy body is woken up and the mind with it.

Making thinking visible in meetings is an important way to assure the quality of thinking that goes on between people who are colleagues and collaborators. Except in the most aware organizations it is not yet common practice. Even then meetings can be so highly political that the last thing people want to do is to reveal what they are really thinking. But where colleagues genuinely want to solve a problem together and where there is a real intention to encourage the best from each other, even then impediments get in the way. Particularly people fear that if meetings are run where thoughts are written down all the time they will be unfree. Although they can accept overtly that thinking is supposed to be under one's control, much of it will be involuntary.

In developing a corporate culture therefore where meetings use visible thinking, there needs to be a freedom for people to just think out loud without fearing that what they say and write is cast in concrete. You need to encourage a special freedom in tearing up something that was written only two minutes before. The symbolic act of destruction of an idea on paper is a stronger retraction than just a verbal withdrawal. You are visibly wiping the slate clean. Another freedom is gained as well. The currency of the meeting is in paper. So because of the contrast when you do not write something down, it appears much more unformed. The spoken word gains a new freedom. Your words can float until you want to form them into something more solid. A space is created in which you can just think out loud. Often then your colleagues will help you formulate your thoughts, participating with you in the effort to ground an elusive idea. There is joint ownership and you are not so isolated. This common ownership is reinforced by the involvement of everyone in writing things down and sticking them up. Entrenched positions are less likely to occur because no one stays fixed in one seat. The movement of people around the room assures surprising exchanges and changes of outlook.

Compared with live meetings, computer networking is more congenial to signalling and labelling thinking processes. It is much closer to deskwork, where people can more readily control their own thinking processes. Real-time meetings require a lot of effort to be devoted to managing the group, ensuring that every member of the meeting participates fully. On computer the effort can be put in by a support system. Let me speculate how it could work. It could comprise several options. One option would offer the Thunks themselves to help in the quality assurance of letters and reports both sent and received. Option two would be maps and subroutines, windowed in when needed in wholes or chunks at different degrees of depth, to remind you where you are going or to review where you have come from. Option three would help you build your own maps and models for new projects, especially those that have system-wide implications. This would be an expert system for thinking about all and everything.

I am not a software expert, and my consulting work has not yet taken me into this realm. In the companies where I am working, in spite of their being among the most advanced in the world, the greater part of the 'brain of the firm' operates through face-to-face contact. Since people are much more careful about what they write or send by computer than about what they say, most of my work on raising the quality of thought has been live. If Thunks and maps were used as expert systems in computers it would help people get hold of the Thunks language faster and speed the facility with which people can then use them live, real-time, with one another. Of course the added nicety is that Thunks themselves can be used to quality assure the programs.

Six Checks on your Thinking

The whole point of conceptual tools is to raise the quality of thinking. Everyone can think but let's face it, we often get by with very sloppy thinking indeed. If it does the job well enough, then people stay fairly sloppy. In my view, most people's standards for thinking are too low and what is considered well enough is usually well below par. You may be getting the impression that I am idealistic. I hope my pragmatic realism is not missed. The company that will survive is the one that quality assures its thinking. No organization I have worked with was more pragmatically realistic than Hoover yet the standards it set were very high. Technical training was meticulous. The Hoover way was an object lesson, even down to wiring a plug with millimetre precision. Customer relations training was demanding. The representative had to be able to enter the homes of millionaires and council house tenants and sell to both. Yet it was these high standards that created the goodwill to network on and sell more machines. Standards were maintained because they brought in more business. High standards, as long as they are the right ones, give a competitive advantage.

It is essential to know when it matters that you meet a high standard of thinking, to raise the game and to think at peak performance level, rather as one takes a quite different attitude to tennis in a tournament than when playing with friends. To raise your game means putting in the practice so that it is possible to achieve a higher performance. Here are six ways to practise.

Sequence and Order

One problem is that, left to operate inside the brain only, thinking seldom seems to come in the right order. Very clever people believe with some truth that they actually can marshal their thoughts with perfect coherence, but sadly they do this at the expense of freedom to use their imagination fully. Analytical and convergent thinking excludes whatever ideas might have come from divergent thinking. Those who pride themselves on thinking in numbered lists are good only for petty bureaucratic tasks and actually have to unlearn this excellent discipline when they need to make a creative contribution.

Luckily it is possible to eat your cake and have it still. The trick is to provide yourself with a range of blank sheets which act as visual thought-collectors. Each one has its own heading so that it will attract only particular kinds of thought. The best form of heading is usually a question which you hope or expect to find answers to. For instance in making a plan, I would have one sheet labelled 'What could go wrong?' and this thought-collecting bin would catch potential threats, whenever they happened to come into anyone's mind in whatever sequence. The order comes not in the sequence in which the thoughts are thought but later when the sheets are reorganized. Where do the headings for these thought-collectors come from? Naturally from one's maps, subroutines and Thunks.

Physical conditions and ways of operating are of immense importance in assuring the quality of thought, whether at one's own desk or in a meeting. It matters a great deal how one recognizes, gathers in and records what comes out of people's minds. Sequence is a real issue and if not managed skilfully will block or choke off ideas and information, or will dump on you a tangled mass of incoherent and disorderly thoughts that might even be too daunting to make use of. Because of this, many thoughts are not even caught and recorded at all, disappearing into the haze of tobacco smoke before being clarified. It's all a waste. Brainstorming is a special case, of course, because one of its key principles is to take whatever comes without judgement. I use brainstorming as part of a process to get exceptional results. I have, therefore, had to develop a methodology for handling its output efficiently. The relevant aspect here is to make yourself independent of sequence in the real-time generating of ideas, and yet to readily organize the output afterwards, without much difficulty and use of time. In the real-time workshops mentioned already, the information is made infinitely flexible, either through moving ideas about physically on chits, five inches by three inches, or by the use of special layouts on flip chart sized paper, which enable you to 'move' information conceptually rather than physically. This Visual Gathering is so named to capture the notion of gathering ideas visually and also holding gatherings that are run by making the proceedings visual. The idea of defeating sequence by making visual thought-buckets and moving them around is so effective that some people are imitating this with software on computers. The mobility of information is a real asset but the most difficult and important aspect of Visual Gathering is the quality of the questioning and structuring. This is where Thunks and maps are so vital.

Direction

When you think, what are you aiming for? Your aim gives you a direction which leads your thinking. The goal mouth attracts the efforts of the players. In football there are two opposing goals. By analogy when you look towards one thinking goal you are not only forsaking the other but actually turning your back on it. The directions are in conflict. The thinking goal I most often want to achieve is to come up with a wonderful new idea. I like to visit the space that is beyond relevance frequently, which then of course produces thoughts that will obviously be different from what is already known and probably will also affront values that are firmly rooted in the past. New ideas are normally rejected by entrenched experts and people who fear the unfamiliar. The direction of my mind will class with others who have stayed inside relevance. This is why it is sometimes hard for a scientist to accept experimental results when they disagree with his hopes and expectations, or raise difficult moral issues. Newspaper publishers and journalists have similar difficulties: to publish what is new(s) (green), what is true (red), or what will appeal (blue)? When you want to quality assure your approach to handle clashes like these you must ask 'What is the goal, and what is the main direction I must go in?' The Orientation Map is of course designed to sort this out. It is a purpose-built map to quality assure direction, to unbundle from the many possible routes the best one to follow.

The other side of fixing your direction is unfixing it. If you know where you are going with your thinking you are more able to sense when your direction is off course and so to switch to a better approach. I vividly remember an occasion when I was invited to make a presentation to a group of planners. I prepared a logical and formal presentation. Half-way in to the live event I felt very uneasy. There was no rapport. I was getting responses that didn't match my direction at all. Then it dawned: the most senior person present was operating from another direction altogether. He wanted to play with ideas, not reach a conclusion. I had subsumed my normal propensity to throw ideas around in the belief that I should follow a sober line of thought. I had got it wrong. On this occasion I didn't manage to rescue myself. There is always a danger that once you commit to a direction, as I said at the beginning, you shut off the other possibilities that might have been more appropriate. Yet you must commit, else nothing moves. The art is to choose, yet remain aware of it as a choice so that it can be changed. There's a cost for not getting it right in the first place. The cost on this occasion for me was that I didn't get a contract.

Workability

Workability means 'reason demands that it should work'. You must check that any kind of thinking routine, sequence or model that you might come across is really workable for you. There are two aspects of this. First, is the tool structurally sound? Is it consistent within itself and in relation to other tools you use? Is the formula right? You need to check the objective relevance of your thinking process, the tool you are intending to use. On most occasions you will probably be checking out something quickly that is jotted on to the back of a used envelope. (I am keen on used envelopes because they provide a firm, chit-sized tool which can be thrown away without compunction if thoughts are wrong, need correcting, or when I have finished with them. Envelopes are such workmanlike tools that 'the back of an envelope' has become a metaphor.) When you check structure you are asking three questions: What's in it that shouldn't be there? What's not in it that should be there? Are the parts soundly related to each other? The second question is often most difficult. By referring to a Thunks array like Figure 3.1, you can spark yourself with ideas for what else should be included. The third question is determined by logic. For instance you shouldn't use Test until you have developed an idea to some depth.

Second, is the tool right for you? Can you work it? When I first got hold of a scythe I couldn't handle it at all, although I had seen it being used with a skill that led me to believe that it could be used to shave with. I admired it as a tool but I never learned how to use it. You must find the tools that work for you. Our constant aim through the Philips project was to encourage managers to take the tools we made and customize them for themselves. Some managers did customize, most did not. There is always a danger of taking what is given without quality assuring it to suit one's own thinking style. Naturally this applies to everything offered in this book. It is such a welcome change when someone adapts a tool to suit his mind and job, for example clothing generic questions with data that makes them more cogent for his work.

Balance

By balance I do not want to imply that thinking should be evenly balanced. Switching from one task to another involves switching the balance of your approach from Ideas Thunks, to Information Thunks, to Judgement Thunks. I have to keep a constant eye on my own tendency to over-use one set of Thunks, the green ones, in an unbalanced way. People often devote too much effort to one aspect of thinking, leaving too little space for the others. Their thinking styles are far more constant than they would suppose, as my observations on managers at work have shown. They have a tendency to bring the same limited sequences of Thunks to every task, whether it is appropriate or not. This is most marked in western educated groups of managers, who trap their thinking within relevance.

Sadly it is all too common for executives in business or in government to reach decisions in a totally unbalanced way. For instance the hard-nosed professional manager might have deluded himself into believing that decisions should be made entirely objectively, with no room for subjective values and interpretations. The mechanistic disciplines of engineering and accountancy are well known for this lacuna. Some unlucky people discover this only later in life when they retire. They feel as if the lid is being taken off and they can use the whole of themselves at last. And almost by definition it is 'irrelevant' creative thinking that is needed when the situation you face is 'impossible', when you wish to gain a competitive edge, when you have ambitions for excellence or market leadership, or when all normal approaches have already failed.

To quality assure the balance of my own thinking plans when there is no time to run through all the Thunks I use the colour-frame below as a quick checklist. My purpose is to determine where the emphasis should be. The balance sometimes might be tilted towards communication, getting a message across, or making sure to really hear what is going on. Sometimes the balance might be in seeking ingenious thoughts or even visionary ones, or being willing to just wait for them to come from other people, well tilted towards the green. Another check is whether the plan is top-heavy on hard or weighted down with soft.

Workability	Knowledge	Ingenuity
Value	Communication	Vision

Level

One of the most common reasons for being off the mark is operating on the wrong level or scale. Coupled with this, though sufficiently important to devote the following section to it as well, is the level of detailed accuracy. 'How much detail' is not always a function of the amount of time needed or available, or the importance of the issue, but rather to a reading of what is appropriate. Issues that are important might be quite simple. Churchill risked much with his insistence during the Second World War that nothing was so complex and difficult it could not be conveyed to him on one-half of a sheet of paper. It is certainly to be hoped that someone had done his staff-work. There is often no need to go into immense detail in order to reach the right conclusion. On the other hand some kinds of decision can be satisfactorily made only by detailed investigations or persistent probing.

One of the greatest difficulties in decision-making and planning is to determine the level of your goal. Currently I am developing a business plan within a global horizon yet I am wondering whether I should reduce the scope to a European level. What might be good at the global level, having sold the rights of my first book in Japan and Germany, might be counter-productive at the European level. How much should I find out about the Japanese market if I am going global and how much should I bother if I stay European? Possibly I should bother even more! Whatever the scale of business the same issues of level apply.

Among the complaints made by businesses about the British government's handling of the economy is that they never know the planning horizon it is working to. It is anyway always too short, and governments delight moreover in moving the goalposts. In boardroom discussions it is important to be aware whether you are making an operational decision or whether what you commit to will alter the nature and direction of the business in a strategic or policy-making way. It might be objected that implications are not always clear or predictable. All the more reason for doing some quality assurance on the process. For instance when establishing a goal of any kind, has there been any attempt to test it at both the level above and the level below by focusing on causes and effects? When President Bush went into Panama, was this a strategic or an operational decision? When Argentine invaded the Falklands, did they consider that their action might evoke in Britain a response on such a high moral plane? To have made a judgement is one thing. To have not even considered shifting of level means that decisions are made by default. So conceptual tools which deliver checklists of questions that might well be asked are essential for assuring thinking quality. A checklist I find invaluable for setting the level is shown in Figure 7.1.

Accuracy and Completeness

Accuracy needs to be coupled with level and with completeness, although it can be distinguished from both. The combination produces quality of accurate information rather than quantity. Since no one can ever get all the information that could possibly be found, everyone has to make a judgement when to consider it is complete enough to be good enough. Too much can lower the quality, even if all the details are as accurate as $2 + 2 = 4$. You want accuracy that is just good enough. You get it by juggling with level and completeness asking, 'At this level what kind of information will supply a complete enough answer?' The lower the level of your goal, though, the greater the quantity of information needed.

In order to quality assure getting accuracy, the obvious Thunk is Specify. To complement Specify it needs its fellow hard red Thunk,

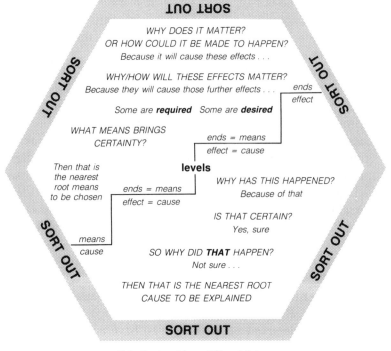

7.1 Sort out Level Checklist

Categorise. To ensure relevance it needs hard blue Distinguish, Compare and Test. To prevent its being trapped in relevance you should call upon Challenge, Escape and Pursue from hard green. There are more tools here to check for accuracy than anyone is likely to use at one time. I therefore pick up only the ones that seem to leap out at me as being appropriate. Perhaps you have experienced how the right cooking implement seems magically to insinuate itself into your hand if you just look at a rack of them. How did you choose it? It chose itself. This is exactly what seems to happen when I look at the Thunks and say 'Now which one?'

To quality assure completeness of gathering information, good process checklists are ideal. You will never reach completeness if you do not get your thinking outside relevance. It is a safe bet that if you have not planned to engage your mind with some of the green Thunks your search for information will be incomplete. You must access sources that seem outside and beyond what is immediately concerned with the problem.

Using Thunks as a Generic Checklist

Quality assuring means being constantly alert and steering your thinking. The earliest tool I can remember using is a mnemonic to remember lists of battles, treaties and so on for history examinations. I also remember being taught a poor relation to brainstorming to get my ideas going for essays. I first met checklists in Hoover to cover service routines. A fellow management trainee was brilliant at putting mnemonics to the checklists so we could remember them without always looking them up. At Rank Xerox, in the swinging sixties, the matrix was a great discovery for me. It was closely followed by concentric circles to show relationships between things at different levels, the most important being in the middle. A remarkable systems analyst in Xerox who couldn't talk or think without a pencil in his hand indelibly imprinted me with the importance of making thinking visible. He inspired me to recognize that I too could make tools and I made my first plunge into the use of layout and design of formats to steer thinking. The joy and fun of each new tool, of feeling my mind stretch and broaden as I made use of it, was a wonderful feeling. One of the most exciting experiences was coming across the Kepner Tregoe (KT) system of tools for rational decision-making. Whenever I get hold of a tool I make it work for me to see its effects, not just on myself but others. My urge is also to put the question, 'Is this complete?' I worked with the KT tools in depth and, as I have explained already, found the system lacked the creative dimension. So in establishing my own consultancy the mission was to research creativity and encourage more of it in organizations.

Looking back from today's vantage point, I can see I was thirsting for integration within myself, so that I could bring together the artistic and creative heritage of my childhood with the formal nature of my education. I had to build unity within myself in order to help others to build it for themselves. At heart I am always returning to my first vocation of teaching; to help others learn better I look for better tools, more complete, more integrated, more human.

So it is not surprising that serendipity brought me into the Philips project. Here was a small team who having looked at all the thinking tools they could lay their hands on were saying, 'The tools are incomplete. They are not an integrated system. For our business we must build something better so that our managers will be advantageously placed to think better.' Because the model of Thunks we built pretends to the status of a total system, all its components can be seen as mutual checks and balances on each other. The layout of the Thunks in Figure 7.2 does attempt to position the Thunks so that some of the dynamics are indicated by proximity to and distance from each other.

I have already shown one case in the previous section where several Thunks can be mobilized to check just one, Specify. Now I will try to illustrate how you can pick one Thunk to amplify or test another, so that in the process of additions and counterchecks between pairs or trios of Thunks you can always quality assure any line of thought you take.

Feel and Observe *versus* Test and Specify

I often get ideas through hunch and intuition from the Thunk Feel. Coming from the world of imagination that requires little evidence there is every reason for checking the idea further. Feel is asking for the soft red support of Observe, the Thunk that invites the use of the information-gathering senses of your whole body. It is no use subjecting Feel to hard blue Test, or even hard red Specify. The quantification and insistence on relevance by these two Thunks would destroy whatever ideas Feel was endeavouring to bring through. Some managers actually pride themselves on the toughness and rigour with which they ignore or crush intuitions, either within their own minds or from a subordinate. The trouble with intuition is that it is sometimes right.

Coupling Observe with Feel will cause you to find out more, to welcome the incoming idea to see if by using all sources of information available the idea can take on substance. Not only looking but also focusing. Not only hearing but actively listening. Getting hold of reality by firsthand experience through as many senses as possible. Some people believe that intuitions are never without evidence, it is simply that one cannot discern the evidence with normal consciousness. So we have to tune in to listen very hard to the weak signals that bring the message in. We must read between the lines and hear the music beyond the obvious. Investigation along normal lines may be inadequate. Just as light rays have force but no mass, so those weak signals may have little substance but you can feel their force. This is what checking out Feel with Observe really means.

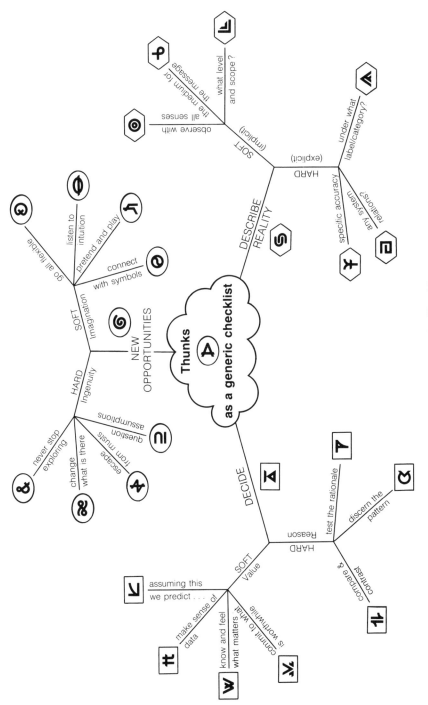

7.2 Thunks as a Generic Checklist

Code with Value

The purpose of using Code in its sender mode is to choose the best way to put something across to a particular targetted audience. How can you ensure the message they receive and understand is as close as possible to the one you intend to convey? They will have a different perceptual base, different history or experience, different hopes and expectations, different reasoning processes, and above all different values, motives, criteria and goals. How you sell successfully to one audience might switch off another entirely. To present a new idea too imaginatively can be death if the audience needs a feeling of safety and reassurance in terms of familiar experience and values. I know far too well that talking to an audience of scientists is very different from talking to training managers or people from the commercial side.

There are several Thunks for checking Code including soft red Set Level, hard red Look in/out, soft green Symbolise and Pretend, and soft blue Interpret. I will contain myself here to Value which helps to think through what makes an audience tick. You must discover their criteria in the context of your presentation. You must know what matters to them, and what approach will make it easy for them to take it in and understand. Remember you are not in the game of changing what you want to say, only how you say it. I am presuming that you are not like the weak politician who creates his policy according to what will please the voters, but that you are concerned with promoting the decision you are committed to and simply wish to ensure it gets the fair wind of understanding. It is not the function of Code to tell lies or to be economical with the truth, but to express a reality effectively. The values of the listener can actually get in the way, can reduce truth or obscure it, can bias what is heard out of all recognition. When some people hear the word 'profit' they shudder with distaste and revulsion, while for others it brings a gleam to the eye. By misreading or not even bothering to study the audience, you might display to them something 'good' as if it were 'bad', especially across boundaries of culture, nationality or race. In choosing between two ways to express a vital point, better to choose the way that resonates sweetly and not discordantly. How can anyone know if he has coded his message well if he cannot show how and why it will be in the language of the listener's values?

Quality Assuring Thunks as a System

Within the confines of this book I can only demonstrate in small part the interconnectedness of the whole system of Thunks. You will find you never use one Thunk on its own for long. Every Thunk needs its mates. Sometimes I play the game of pretending to be cast away on a desert island with only one Thunk. Which one would it be? If I pick a favourite green Thunk, say Symbolise, then suddenly all the world appears to be governed by symbolism. Yes, I could manage if Symbolise was all I had. And so I could with Distinguish. (George Kelly built his construct system on the idea that distinguishing constructs is the key to all human behaviour.) If I proceed through the Thunks I begin to realize that the Thunks are rather like a shattered hologram, each one as a piece of the whole reflects the whole of thought within itself. When I play the opposite game, the game of losing just one Thunk at a time, I see that I can always make do without it by bringing in other Thunks to do the missing one's job. The model acts like the brain which because its design is full of redundancies can compensate for losses. I have played these games with many groups to encourage them to check out the wholeness of the system. It cannot easily be proved that a system like this is whole, but I've had a lot of fun trying to disprove it. So far without success.

Using One Model to Quality Assure Another

How does one really understand the value of someone else's work? How does one critique work done as a result of delegation, or the work of a consultant or an agency or some other subcontractor whom you have briefed? How do you read a report or a book with heightened intelligence, or evaluate a system or a model proposed by some expert? First of all the tool you pick up should be appropriate for the task. This means that you cannot expect too much if you appraise an economic model with a model made for interpersonal behaviour. Nor will you get far in appreciating a model of cognitive behaviour if you use only a model of affective behaviour. There will be some useful insights to be made in all these cases but they are unlikely to be definitive of the whole. On the other hand, any area of expertise with a strong cognitive element repays critique via another cognitive model. Even experts fail to critique the models they are using by cross-referring between them. There are people who have not realized that learning is part of thinking, that lateral thinking represents only a part of creative thinking, and that there are dangerous assumptions embedded even in the powerful concept of rational thinking.

Because of my lifelong interest in learning I am choosing as an example to use the Thunks model to quality assure a couple of learning models via the profiling inventories based on them. Even when covering the same field, namely learning, different profiles will reveal different dynamics. Managers are often surprised when a profile revealed by one model differs from that revealed by another. It seems to them rather like the old story of the stationmaster in Ireland who, when the bishop complained that the clock in the booking hall told a different time from the clock on the platform, explained that there was no point in having two clocks if they both told the same time. Portraits of people and their minds are not like clocks, however. There will usually be a recognizable overlap between two or more profiles of the same person but no perfect correlation, otherwise why use more than one profile? One profile of the complex task of learning will inform the description given by another, so I will use the analysis of two learning inventories to suggest a promising means of critique and appreciation.

The Honey–Mumford Learning Styles Questionnaire is based on the model originated by Kolb and others, and written up in the book *Organization Psychology: An Experimental Approach* (D. A. Kolb, I. M. Rubin, J. M. McIntyre, Prentice-Hall, Englewood Cliffs, NJ, 1974) which described learning as a cycle of four stages. By showing the abstract-concrete parameter as intersecting the active-passive parameter at 90 degrees, a model of four apparently equal quadrants was formed. I say apparently because I have serious doubts the four aspects are equidistant. A very short inventory of single words typical of each of the four offered a profile of people's learning styles. Several useful contrasts could be readily established between the four aspects, based on the four arms of the model or the quadrants between, and comparing the upper with the lower half or the left with the right.

Peter Honey and Alan Mumford in the UK focused on the quadrants of the cycle which they named Activist, Reflector, Theorist and Pragmatist (Honey and Mumford, *The Manual of Learning Styles*, Peter Honey, 1982). They also developed a more substantial questionnaire but this should not be expected to produce scores that correlate with those of Kolb because the inventories come from different angles. Yet it is possible to miss the difference between the two models and inventories without some form of quality assurance scrutiny. This might not matter much because both are useful models and any given manager is unlikely to experience both and so will not be confused. What interested me is that when asked to investigate these models by a client organization who were concerned about authenticity of results, I put them through a simple test as far as possible. I checked through each inventory with the Thunks. In the case of Kolb I could not recognize many of the one-word behavioural elements of the inventory in terms of the cognitive operations defined by Thunks and I was forced to abandon the idea as too difficult. For me that says something significant. Let me show you the results I got on the 80 questions in the Honey–Mumford inventory. I found that the six colours of thinking were represented roughly in the following proportions:

Hard Blue 25%	Hard Red 20%	Hard Green 16%
Soft Blue 11%	Soft Red 20%	Soft Green 8%

This gives a crude but interesting profile of the distribution of thinking-force measured by this inventory. More fascinating was finding that out of 80 questions, 64 were reflecting the operation of only eight Thunks, and that as far as I could see some ten Thunks are barely represented at all. To say this may not constitute an adverse criticism of the inventory, rather it reveals what this inventory considers is important and unimportant in the learning process. The point is that one can now understand and appreciate the merits of the Honey–Mumford inventory as seen through the Thunks, and question how far it reflects the whole learning process adequately for one's purposes.

The eight Thunks most used in the Honey–Mumford Questionnaire were

Observe	12 times	Soft Red
Test	11	Hard Blue
Specify	10	Hard Red
Distinguish	8	Hard Blue
Value	8	Soft Blue

Escape	5	Hard Green
Unform	5	Soft Green
Categorise	5	Hard Red

An inventory of a different kind is Michael Kirton's KAI which offers a quick discrimination between people who manage their approach to change in an Adaptive or an Innovative way (Kirton, *Adaptors and Innovators*, Routledge, 1989). These polarities are on a continuum, and the scores on that single line help to show how creative or conservative people are. Putting the inventory through a similar quality assurance test reveals this distribution:

Hard Blue 24%	Hard Red 38%	Hard Green 20%
Soft Blue 6%	Soft Red 2%	Soft Green 10%

I would like to propose that the Thunks model could be used as a meta model for examining all thinking tools and disciplines. If the cross-fertilization between chemistry, physics, biology, mathematics and philosophy is to flower, a common language of thought is needed which transcends the differences of jargon and tradition. For management and the brain-workers of our times, their jobs will be immeasurably enhanced with a meta model of thought.

8

Conceptual Learning

'The more I learns, the less I seems to know.' Am I just getting worse and worse, or could my standards be rising? One of my golden memories is of the laboratory chief who stood up at the end of a week-long management development course on thinking skills. He made a little speech of thanks and then produced a card with a big letter L, which he proudly glued on to his forehead. Here was a man of some standing, highly respected by his fellow scientists, proclaiming himself now a Learner-driver. It was not only humility but the deep insight of an experienced manager. He had the imagination to realize that a new field had opened up for him to develop. He had conceptualized what he had 'learned' by his participation with his colleagues, and seen that there would be wide applications which were now only just at their beginning. Real learning would take place over the following months and years. By contrast, it is still commonplace, even for quite experienced people running management development courses, to attempt a so-called course evaluation at the end of it. In their anxiety to get feedback, those course directors may be risking sending an entirely counter-productive signal to the participating managers: 'It is all over now, boys. You have passed the test and you can chuck your L-plate away and get on with the real business of driving your work.' What a shame!

What is Learning?

The point of learning is to profit from experience, to make experience useful. Just to kick off, there are so many ways to look at learning, according to what is being learnt and why. It matters whether you see the purpose as to add, subtract, divide or multiply. Adding knowledge is perhaps the most common image, characterized by ask, tell and see. By adding experience and knowledge you enrich your own database from which you can later conceptualize your learning. This is why I believe so strongly that children need a wide range of experiences in their early lives so that they have more to build on in adulthood. So naturally I argue against a narrowing down into job-related training during school education. Our children need all the wealth of the sciences and the visual arts, literature, drama and music, athletics and sport, crafts and languages, to develop all their thinking capacities and provide the storehouse of experience from which their imagination (green Thunks), values and judgement (blue Thunks), and sensitivities (red Thunks) can mature. Adding to this wealth is not sufficient on its own, but provides the essential base on which conceptual development can blossom.

Subtracting means unlearning, an often uncomfortable feeling of having conclusions tested or assumptions challenged. This is normally a process adults have to face once formal education has finished, and learning just through living takes over. Every time you have to get rid of a habit of mind or body, of attitude or behaviour, you are unlearning. The longer the habit has been there the harder to remove. The easiest way to replace it is by overwhelming it with a stronger stream. So smokers switch to chewing gum. Moving to a greenfield site is an easier route to unlearning outmoded organization habits than sticking in the same place and trying to bring about change. If you are seeking to remove a habit by your own conscious will, a rewarding though tough demand on one's self-discipline, then the Thunks to use are Challenge (the old) and Test (the new). With Challenge you invite yourself to stop and think before your habit takes its course and with Test you check what alternative action you are about to take. One of the most useful methods for tackling habit of mind and body is the Alexander Technique.

Division is often done by analysis and routinizing, as ways of reducing work. Work study and O & M are the archetypes. Such division actually creates habits, automatic patterns for managing tasks efficiently. So it is essential to link division with subtraction, in a constant alertness to the danger of building habits without also caring for removing them when they are no longer wanted or needed. Division is also the process of concentrating experience into nuggets of wisdom and understanding. Trainers need to be exceptionally good at this, distilling best practice from many fields to build programmes in which training for excellence is done in a condensed learning period. What they do is identify generic patterns (theory), and then clothe them in user-friendly teaching and learning methods to get the message across. Training based on 'division' is fast, extremely cost-effective and very different from the education process of 'addition' which requires extended time periods in which experiences can be repeated, savoured and digested. If learning by division is to be effective it needs a sound base on which to work. 'Trainees' need the richness of a broad education so that they can respond from their own life's experience to the concentrated dose of 'division learning'.

Multiplying means expanding the usefulness of what's learned, conceiving many applications from the core patterns discerned by division. To be able to recognize what has actually been learned for transfer to different-yet-similar situations is of critical importance, and thus a part of the learning process. It requires both the skilful use of the logical Thunk Distinguish on one's observation of experience, and the use of one or more of the green Thunks of imagination. When something has been learned, you can do it again when something similar is faced, and this accounts for people who think of learning as memorizing, just adding. Multiplying is 'learning to do it again', but to something else that is different-and-yet-similar. So if I can throw a stone, I can throw another, and also a cricket ball and also . . . and there's the rub: what else is similar? Are there things I cannot throw, by virtue of throwing a stone, well? Could I really throw a javelin, which has such a different shape? Oddly enough, a good cricket-ball thrower is very likely to throw a javelin far, because what is different-and-yet-similar is the throwing, not the object. In contrast he is not likely to be so readily successful with the shot-put because although the shot looks round like the cricket ball it demands throwing skills of quite a different kind.

People who remain literalist about their experience restrict their learning severely, stuck in relevance. Managers frequently fail to recognize the value of experience in one field when they deal with something apparently worlds away from it. They cannot connect with what is common to both. They do not see how someone from a different industry can possibly manage their own. They cannot connect what happened in an outdoors training course with the way to create teamwork in their office. They will not look to another discipline to inform their own specialism, and so on.

Self-awareness is Critical for Learning

If you are unaware of how you are doing something, regardless of whether it is being done badly or exceptionally well, you will be unable to learn from it and translate it to other fields. The natural athlete is a classic example of someone who can perform exceptionally without knowing how. Until he discovers what he does he cannot improve himself. Being self-aware is critical if one is to build further on whatever one has learned. This ability to transfer is a multiplier. The trouble is, not only does it require awareness but also more skills of abstraction and conceptualization than some people are willing to develop. I suspect that much of the learning that people take from training programmes is never acknowledged because they haven't conceptualized their previous state of knowledge and skill and therefore cannot identify what has changed in themselves.

One of the important roles of a coach is to increase the athlete's awareness of his own performance. Even if the coach cannot perform so magnificently as his charge, he knows what it feels like and has above all the observant eye. In just a few companies there are people who are fulfilling this role of observer with managers, sitting at their elbow or acting as facilitators in certain meetings. There has to be some way for a manager to give himself feedback before he can learn. It's extremely difficult to concentrate on what you are doing in trying to get a result and at the same time to watch yourself, without spoiling what you do. It's as if as soon as your inner camera begins to roll, it affects what you do in front of it. I remember a beautiful piece of real film footage which we had in the Oxford University Athletic Club, which showed one of our own members running down the back straight in a demonstration of perfect style. He was at that time one of the best athletes in the world and his style happened also to be remarkably fluid and well co-ordinated. Here he was, striding down the track with his left arm going forward with his left leg and his right arm going forward with his right. . . If you try it, you will see the joke.

During the course of a busy day at work it is only sometimes possible to get others to give you feedback from which you can decipher your own learning needs. Models and maps are, in effect, feedback systems and can be used to help yourself become more aware of your own learning needs. Taking this thought further, if you are serious about developing your own thinking skills, the most effective method for pushing yourself on is to teach or coach someone else. It is my considered view that one learns most by teaching. Teaching means helping someone else to learn. This is much harder than just learning for yourself. It involves becoming so conscious and explicit about the models and maps that form in one's own mind that they can be shared with someone else who has a quite different model-forming resource in his mind. One cannot foist just any model on to someone else if he is unable to recognize and have a feeling for it. This is the age-old problem of communication: it takes two to tango. You have to start from where the other person is and build the conceptual bridge from your models to his so that you can together share the same one. This does not mean abandoning a model that works just because it is only in your own head. It is all too easy to focus so much on the needs of the receiver of a message that the needs of its sender are totally ignored. In fact it may be the very difference between your model and his that accelerates his learning, and yours.

In our age of information we all have to be teachers to each other to keep pace with the changes that information so rapidly forces. Such teaching *inter pares* requires us to be conceptually alert and skilful with models and maps. I use models to explain *why* I see and approach things the way I do, and maps to show *how* to do something. Models are more abstract, maps more concrete, but both are conceptual. (See Figure 2.1 as a reminder.) When people teach one another they express their understanding of their own experiences and describe them in words and diagrams. What would otherwise remain largely unconscious then becomes conceptualized. Once you start explicating an experience you have to shape it into a model of some kind in order to formulate what you want to pass on to someone else. The more the manager teaches his staff the conceptual insights of his experience, the richer and stronger grows his own mental modelling and mapping. While others benefit, so does he. His teaching fuels his own development as a conceptual manager.

The methodology of the colours and Thunks not only helps the teaching–learning process within the models and maps already shown in the book, but also gives insight into the very processes of learning and teaching themselves. This can be approached from several angles, but let me start from here: learning is to do with achieving a conscious match that is better than before between intentions and action. Happiness is actually doing what reflects your intentions. What could be more appropriate than to approach learning through a better understanding of intentions?

Learning Styles

I have already said several times that the model of Thunks is a new concept, in that it shows what the mind *intends* to think. It is a model of potential mental energy, at the 'Ready' for thoughts of all kinds. The mind moves to 'Get set' in the Orientation Map, and to 'Go' when committed to a particular thinking plan based on a map like Selling or Decision-making. When you actually start thinking through the plan, then you are moving from potential thinking into thought itself. Intention runs into thought. For knowledge workers and for managers, thought is action. A schema of maps, like New Achievement in Figure 4.1, is designed to draw thinking intention and thought-action closer together, so that action matches intention.

While the maps are designed for getting intentions lined up with the task 'out there', the model of Thunks, on which the maps are based, shows what is 'inside' people's minds. The model displays all the mental operations a person is potentially capable of using. In order to learn, all these mental operations at some time or another will be brought into play. Wouldn't it therefore be useful to consider Thunks as the means for modelling learning? This is in fact what I started to do back in 1984 with the development of the Thunks profiling instrument.

There are already several methods available for profiling learning styles. Kolb's Learning Styles Inventory has gained widespread usage and Honey–Mumford's Learning Styles Questionnaire, drawn from Kolb, has also proved useful. These instruments are based on the learning cycle which I described in Chapter 7. I want to propose here that the model of Thunks is more thorough and robust than the learning cycle for understanding the elements of learning, and that my profile of thinking intentions (TIP), based on the model of Thunks, is an incisive tool for predicting learning styles. My argument is that how someone learns has a great deal to do with his thinking style.

The Thinking Intentions Profile (TIP) is a preference inventory for measuring thinking styles. It presents 24 questions inviting choice apparently between three ways of thinking. All of the 72 options represent Thunks, and the inventory is so constructed that it reveals which thinking operations are preferred to which others. The results can be shown either at the strategic level of the six colours (blue, red and green in hard and soft) or at the tactical level of Thunks. The inventory has been used by several thousand managers, and we have been able to observe many of those managers closely in learning situations of various kinds. The inventory is used principally as a development tool to help people identify which parts of their thinking are favoured and often used, and which neglected, and how this impacts the way they work on tasks and with people. One such task is the task of learning. Hence the thinking profile reveals your natural and preferred learning style.

What do I mean? The thinking profile shows how anyone likes to use their thinking to tackle any task, including the task of learning. So your profile will also predict your preferred learning style, just as it predicts people's decision style, planning style and so on. This becomes obvious when you watch managers working together on a new activity, when they are busy learning as well as doing, learning how to get on with new people, learning new data and operating with new processes. On programmes and workshops I have watched many hundreds planning how to get results, using feedback to steer their thinking, making good or bad use of their energies, and so on and observed their profiles in action. Working in groups to solve problems, their effectiveness can be seen to grow even in the course of a one week programme of management development. At the beginning, they typically fail, not only to work out how to work well with the others who are probably strangers but especially to sort out their own approach to the task. The behaviour and effectiveness of groups are significantly a function of the mix of thinking/learning styles in each. The course director, by allocating people of particular profiles to different groups, can predict how tasks will be tackled.

In order to observe people's thinking/learning styles live in real-time workshops and to compare with the TIP profiles I use the colour-frame (described in Chapter 3), with the key learning operations identified as follows:

prove it	analyse it	explore it
want it	experience it	conceptualize it

Learning needs all Six Colours

Each person's preference profile from TIP can be superimposed on this colour-frame, so that every individual can identify which colours and Thunks he leads his learning with. Our TIP database shows us that most UK managers drive their thinking and thus their learning from 'prove it'. A read-out from our database puts the sequence of their preferences thus:

1st	4th	6th
2nd	3rd	5th

Resistance to new ideas is the besetting sin of British managers and this profile shows why: their need to have a new idea proved. By definition what is new is always difficult to prove, until it is used. But so many organizations never give an idea a chance. Because they drive their thinking through 'prove it' they often make the mistake of beginning with it. I would argue that 'prove it' should be a step one takes later in working with something new rather than at first.

Unless you are an automaton, everything you do is a learning activity, and therefore the TIP profile is at a deep level the learning profile for all tasks. The sooner people who are learning know their thinking/learning profile the better. It explains to them why they operate as they do – and why another colleague comes from a different angle altogether. Working with this awareness means they learn how to handle their own learning energy, and those of others. This awareness is specially focused through maps. It is no longer just a matter of collaboration through interactive skill and appreciation. It becomes a common recognition of what the task requires, how it should be dealt with, what disciplines have to be applied for effective despatch of the problem. The beauty of it is that the managers involved can recognize the anatomy of the task in the same terms as they now use to recognize the anatomy of their own minds. A learning map, like the one I will suggest in this chapter (Figures 8.1 and 8.2) can help them do so, on another level. They know that if they feel the need to 'prove it', then they must use hard blue Thunks and expect answers that suit hard blue. If they want to know what experiencing it feels like, they must use soft red and actually observe, feel, listen, touch, taste and so on. And if they cannot see the potential for an idea, they might do worse than go to the green Thunks.

For any task they face, it is always open to managers to shift to the higher level of watching themselves struggling with the task and striving to learn how to deal with it. Most of the time, they will be far more concerned about getting results on the task than any learning they might get as a spin-off. Yet sometimes it is worth it to stop and look, not just at the task facing one, but at oneself and one's approach to it. It is a fallacy that we learn by experience: we learn by observing that experience in the light of what we were trying to do, what should have happened, what we might have done, and drawing useful conclusions from all these. Of course, the whole chapter on quality assuring your thinking is about learning to develop your thinking. When we learn we have made a new connection with reality. Sometimes it will be a connection only between things 'out there', or between immediate events, and there is a level of conceptualizing which is sufficient for the immediate purpose only. But the value of conceptualizing comes through when the connection is made with a whole range of applications. And it is fully realized when the learner connects inside himself, when he is aware of what he has learned. 'I've got it . . . I do it . . . I have become it . . . I am now someone different, and I know the way I am changed.'

Learning seems to work in three different if merging intensities, that can be characterized:

(a) I've got it → (b) I do it → (c) I have become it

'I've got it' is as if you have reached out and gathered in all the content so that you have it in a big pouch within you. This is akin to the old image of the teacher opening the lid of one's head and pouring in the contents of the subject. Given that knowledge, you are enabled.

'I do it' involves actually using what's been learned. This sounds trite until one remembers it means that you are so committed to what you have learned that you are willing to actually do something about it. This sort of learning has gone in deeper than merely being enabled. In practice, this degree of willingness applies to an alarmingly small fraction of all that one thinks one has 'learned'. It involves mustering real energy for it, so as to put the learning out into the world in a proactive way. As I will reinforce later, this points up the force of soft blue Thunks in the learning process.

'I have become it' is obviously even more profound. The learning has entered into the very bloodstream so that it has actually transformed the learner himself. It is so much a part of him, he may even be unconscious of its influence. The learning has become autonomic. It is an observable phenomenon that sometimes the learning that is begun during a management development programme can over a period develop in its user so effectively that he will even deny that he learned anything there. Yet a comparison of his actions in the years before and after says something quite else. Of course this hardly ever happens without his having taken an active part over some period in making use of what he had part-learned for his own purposes and in his own way. What is fascinating is that he can quite lose sight of the source of his inspiration. This is a well-established syndrome in the field of evaluating training during the years after taking part in some formal programme. Observation by colleagues on the ground can be far more authentic than questionnaires and surveys.

This suggests a fourth kind of learning statement: (d) 'I have become someone different and what's more I know the way in which I am changed.' This is pretty rare. It certainly requires a conceptual manager to realize that sort of learning, and someone with a fair amount of inner courage, to say so. However, the more he teaches and coaches by forming his own patterns, models, pictures and images to communicate living ideas to others, the more likely he is to reach this kind of understanding.

I hope I have made the case satisfactorily to the reader that how someone learns has a great deal to do with his thinking style. So much so that it is entirely proper to call the Thinking Intentions Profile (TIP) an instrument for predicting how people learn, in other words a learning style questionnaire. Not that it was designed for that purpose. TIP was to give people an insight into their management thinking as a whole, of which learning is an integral part. Alongside TIP, the colour-frame has become a tool for sequencing the emphasis and importance of different phases of learning. (The use of the colour-frame for these processes is described in Chapter 3.) For example, learning foreign languages would be different from learning how to counsel people in distress or learning seamanship. (Although at a high level they all have things in common.) The colour-frame thus becomes a very useful and extremely simple tool for enabling you to identify the essential elements of learning for different kinds of tasks. For instance I use it as the basis for analysing jobs for recruitment, selection and assessment, as well as training and development. Of course the six boxes of the frame are given depth by the Thunks within them so that analysis does not become simplistic.

However, since I do not advocate putting anyone into any one colour-frame, straitjacket, or even a cycle of learning, I have made a map of learning (Figures 8.1 and 8.2), leaving it open to anyone to take whatever pathway he wants through it. Different learning tasks will require a different progress through the map and people with different profiles will take different routes too. I would however caution against following a pathway that matches one's own thinking preferences too closely. This might well be very comfortable, but not necessarily effective for the task.

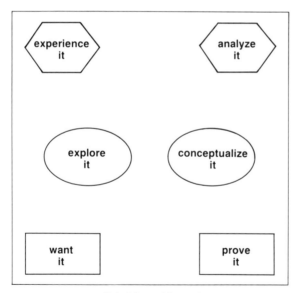

8.1 Map of Learning

A New Learning Map

This map is new, indeed still under development. But I am showing the map in its current form at time of writing, to offer the opportunity for interested readers to help us improve on it, and for others to

EXPERIENCE IT

◎ Let's try, show me, let me do it, alert to all senses

ⅼ Choose the scale of the learning-spiral

ⅎ Tune in the message to my own style

ANALYZE IT

⅄ Methodical, specific questions on detailed facts and figures

⅍ Record all answers, organize in memory so as to copy again

⅂ Put in context, outside/inside, and with what is not so

EXPLORE IT

⊇ Challenge accepted wisdom, habits, assumptions

♯ Make a virtue of difficulties through a winning paradox

æ Being agile and ingenious in new angles and perceptions

& Pursuing curiosity for a better way, a further use

CONCEPTUALIZE IT

Θ Image the result you ideally want

⊖Ə Be open for anything, even dreams and intuition

ƛ Exploit hypotheses and simulations

Ə Leaps of imagination and analogy find elusive connections

WANT IT

W Why it matters: goals worth the sacrifice and effort

Ľ Trust in teacher, risks, estimates and predictions

ᵗᵗ Keen to interpret, understand and evaluate

ᴟ Will reject and stop, get started and commit to use

PROVE IT

⊣ⱶ Make measurements, sound comparisons and contrasts

Ɑ Find the pattern, rules, and principles that make it work

Ⴀ Test the evidence for relevance, probability, validity

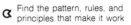

8.2 Thunks Map of Learning

appreciate what is involved in creating a definitive conceptual map. There may be no such thing, but we learn a lot in the trying. One way to do this is to assemble all one knows about learning, including of course the practical experience and the theoretical writings of everyone in sight, and try to find the coherent pattern which best suits one's purpose. Let the universities do that: they are ideally placed for it. My purpose is to arrive at a working tool without further delay, because it is something wanted by the conceptual manager right now, and even more urgently needed by all others. They, especially the conceptual managers, can treat it as a learning tool, improving on it, and learning more about how to learn by using it. This map will have the advantage of being built from the same components as the other maps here, that is Thunks, thus facilitating transfer and connection with management work. Since the work of management is mainly conceptual, maps based in the same language of Thunks are mutually reinforcing.

I have made several versions of this map, and chosen the example in Figures 8.1 and 8.2 because it is so obviously based on the colour-frame that you have already seen. While a map normally has a mix of different coloured Thunks in each step, this one has Thunks all of the same colour in each step. This makes each element or step unusually stark to demonstrate clearly what kind of learning energy is involved. It might turn out that learning is such a high level activity that it really does deserve a set of diverse maps on a lower level, in other words a schema of learning maps. This could be a useful conceptual point to gain from it.

Unless you can be exceptionally self-aware and self-disciplined, any map you initially make will tend to be biased by your own thinking profile – whether you actually prefer to learn via judgement, information or through ideas. The way you value each of the colours and Thunks in general terms is liable to rub off on the way you value the specific task, in this case, learning. For instance, my emphasis when I made my first maps of learning was heavily biased to the green Thunks, because my natural learning style favours them. An example is in Figure 8.3. Note how the map is dominated by green ellipses. My approach to learning something even as basic as tying a knot is to use analogy (the green Thunks Symbolise and Pretend) – the end of the string becomes a water-rat, the loop a pool, the length of string a tree, and a story forms to guide me through the procedure of tying a bowline knot.

Having reflected for a number of years I am now putting forward Figures 8.1 and 8.2 as a more balanced map of learning. The map is a development of the learning colour-frame, spelt out in less abstract and more usable form. Each step fulfils a need or goal, and responds to a difficulty. In walking through the map now I am not suggesting this is the only route, but a useful one.

Experience it

Observe: Let's try, show me, let me do it, alert to all senses
Set Level: Choose the scale of the learning-spiral
Code: Tune in the message to my own style

You must experience something before you can know it: indeed one meaning of the word 'know' is to experience, as in carnal knowledge.

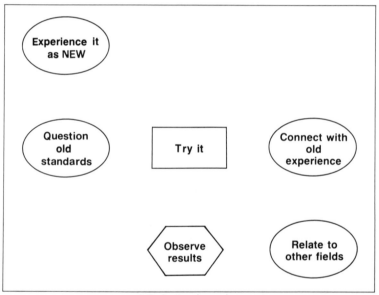

8.3 Active Learning

'We learn by doing', by physical involvement at many levels. Vicarious experience is actually viable, but draws hugely on imagination as a substitute for the engagement of one's own senses. Since this is so well known, it is surprising how many people will show you how to do something difficult, rather than take the conceptually more demanding route of inviting you to find out for yourself and then help you with questions that enable you to think out how to do it. Try it next time your neighbour asks to borrow your lawn-mower and see if you start showing him how to operate it rather than handing it to him with the question 'How do you think it works?'

Want it

Value: Why it matters: goals worth the sacrifice and effort
Predict: Trust in teacher, risks, estimates and predictions
Interpret: Keen to interpret, understand and evaluate
Commit: Will reject and stop, get started and commit to use

You must want to learn enough to provide the energy to start and keep going, to overcome the pain of throwing out old and cherished ways, and to support you when it's difficult or simply hard work. Learning cannot always be fun. It is often challenging and sometimes requires sustained diligence. The motivation that fuels the learner can be extrinsic or intrinsic: he may want to learn because of some great reward if he succeeds, or because the learning itself is its own reward, that is, the subject is of such compelling interest to him. One is doubly lucky when both apply, and I am sure that the huge efforts sustained by some top executives could only be accounted for because their work is their consuming passion and also the demands of the market-place drive them to be always learning. As an aside, the learning cycles of Kolb and Honey–Mumford do not appear to cater enough for motivation.

Explore it

Challenge: Challenge accepted wisdom, habits, assumptions
Escape: Make a virtue of difficulties through a winning paradox
Re-describe: Being agile and ingenious in new angles and perceptions
Pursue: Pursuing curiosity for a better way, a further use

It is sheer curiosity that impels the child to be such an eager learner. He wants to find new things just for the love of it. How sad when quite young men and women (young fogies) seem to have lost it. The drive to explore is also to find an easier way to do the impossible: it's a question of seeking to justify more ambitious goals or standards by finding unusual short-cuts to them. If one were to learn in a more straightforward way, it might remain too difficult. So you look for new angles or ways to 'cheat the system' by finding a pathway not pursued by everyone else.

Analyze it

Specify: Methodical, specific questions on detailed facts and figures
Categorise: Record all answers, organize in memory so as to copy again
Look in/out: Put in context, outside/inside, and with what is not so.

The gathering and analysis of data is perhaps the most obvious aspect of learning, especially where what has to be learned can be seen as 'knowledge', rather than for instance the learning of a skill, the changing of values or the embrace of a new vision. But the need for this element goes farther. Data is not in itself useful unless it is selected by the right questions or until it is otherwise converted into information. Nor is it much good until organized and accessible. So this step makes experience more useful.

Prove it

Compare: Make measurements, sound comparisons and contrasts
Distinguish: Find the pattern, rules and principles that make it work
Test: Test the evidence for relevance, probability, validity

Since by definition one can only learn what one hasn't got, what is new or unfamiliar, then whatever is learned invariably needs proof before taking it on board, or it might be spurious or wrong. It must be tested to ensure it deserves to work, and it is natural to do this mentally before trying something out in the flesh, which could be both risky and costly. Few people are willing to learn anything for which there is no rational explanation.

Conceptualize it

Symbolise: Image the result you ideally want
Feel/Unform: Be open for anything, even dreams and intuition

Pretend: Exploit hypotheses and simulations
Symbolise: Leaps of imagination and analogy find elusive
                  connections

Finally, until something is conceptualized, what is being learned cannot be applied, and worse still cannot be transferred to anything else. Just as the subjective judgement implied in prediction actually goes beyond the straightforward extrapolation of existing trends, so conceptualization goes beyond the rational recognition of the logical patterns in the facts. Imagination in the shape of hypothesis enables patterns to be formed before they are technically justifiable; and in the shape of analogy it enables connections to be made that would not ordinarily be predicted or intended. So conceptualizing is both an enabling function and one that multiplies the applications and the usefulness of whatever is being learned.

While I have made many kinds of learning map there is scope for others, each for a different purpose. One day, we might know enough to arrive at a formula that includes them all. Meanwhile any map can be quality assured in three simple ways. First, have any Thunks been ignored altogether, and if so does it matter? Are there aspects of learning that might not be covered at all? Second, have all the relevant questions available for a particular Thunk been raised? Third, what is the relative balance between the six elements in the map? Where is the real nub of learning? Which are the central elements of the system?

I hope the reader who is interested will take up these questions and come back with challenges and suggestions for improvements. The difficulty of a map is that it cannot include everything. The art is selecting what is most useful and truthful. The choices make a huge difference to the kind of learning that the map will encourage. A nineteenth century schoolteacher might have given a learning map quite a different shape from the one in Figure 8.1 where the two green elements are seen as central. And a computer engineer might adopt a different set of learning priorities from those of an entrepreneurial director. The laying out of the map has some symbolic significance too, influencing or reflecting the kind of thinking process its user will adopt. My original map, Active Learning, formed five years ago was nearly all green, and I had to face up to it that my thinking bias saw learning as a green adventure.

Before leaving this map, you should remember that a map dictates no sequence of thinking operations. Each person taking it up must decide that for himself, in the light of the situation he is facing. These are not single-route maps, but pictures of thought process which show the stages that must be visited, probably with many feedback loops, and the kind of outcomes to expect from each place. They provide a means of knowing where you are in your thinking, and therefore of steering accordingly. Where a 'teacher' is involved, he and the 'learner' had better be in the same place and going in the same direction. Figure 8.4 illustrates this three-way concept. To have a map of learning agreed helps the efficiency and effectiveness of the process.

The Model of Learning and Forming Patterns

One of the most glaring difficulties I have noticed among people engaged in learning is the strong drive either to close down their

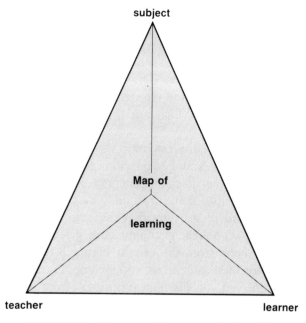

8.4 Unifying Conceptual Language for Learning

minds (blue Thunks) or to open them out (green Thunks): Liam Hudson's convergers and divergers (Hudson, *Frames of Mind*, Penguin, 1968). In/out is a basic thinking pattern, and one is little use without the other. So I've used this as a simple model of the learning process. The movement in Figure 8.5 reads from left to right. At the input end, what you already know is seen as the source of learning objectives, whose selection is a convergent process. At once there is a need to explore as widely as possible in all directions, and this divergence produces new knowledge to be specified and analysed. There follows the essential process of digestion, synthesis, evaluation and other forms of judgement, converging on commitment to whatever gets through this mangle. Then the mind opens again so as to conceptualize the idea beyond its normal relevance, finding connections and applications of various kinds. The model can, of course, be colour-coded, not possible unfortunately in this black and white text. Bear in mind also that this linear model is full of invisible feedback loops.

Central to learning is the creation of patterns in experience. Every pattern, like this model, has an input and an output, and the truly effective learner is the one who makes best use of both. Input and output demand thinking energies that are quite opposite, convergent and divergent as indicated above. So some people are better at the input phase and others at the output. Taking the input first involves finding what is common to many diverse experiences and embodying them all in a single concept at a higher level. Discerning what unites these and distinguishes them from comparable experiences is the function of the hard logical Thunk, Distinguish. Such convergent thinking was the major input to the Philips project for reaching the final forms of the Thunks. If you recall from the story of the Thunks in Chapter 3, our process was to collect and distil experiences from life and phrases from language. We clustered thousands into hundreds, and reduced hundreds into a few dozen and then into the 25 Thunks.

The output end from the pattern is to realize how many other uses there could be for it. If the connections made are pretty obvious, immediate or relevant, then the transfer and multiplication of the learning will be limited. To really exploit the output end shows what conceptualizing can achieve. You need both a clear logical grasp of your pattern, and then the kind of mind that rejoices in finding and making connections that are unusual or remote. This divergent thought is perhaps most fully expressed in the Thunk, Symbolise. From the Philips project we conceptualized the applications of Thunks into many forms of management tools. Even then, ten years

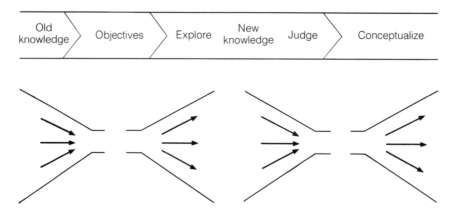

8.5 A Learning Model

ago, we opened out our minds to their uses beyond management in business, to children at school and in the home, athletes and performers, the Open University and so on. Can I conceptualize farther afield? What about the University of the Third Age? What about the Russian mixed-nationality space programme? Would it be useful for 5th generation computers and artificial intelligence? Maybe it could form the basis of a new music or a new dance form? How about using it in penal reform, for fusing the advanced and underdeveloped worlds, for ecumenism within Christianity and beyond, for ecological issues and the uniting of spiritual and material values. Far-fetched? Yes, conceptualizing is letting your mind expand into the wide vistas of the improbable where you may harvest a wealth of outputs from even a small clutch of input.

When I started up my consultancy in the mid-seventies, I remember the moment when I fully realized for the first time that learning and creative conceptualizing had so much in common. On the way home from the Experimental Psychology department where I was doing some of my research in Oxford, coincidentally just as I was passing Rhodes House, I nearly fell off my bicycle as the idea struck me. Of course I was not the first to see it, and in fact Jerome Bruner was then working in that very Psychology department. But any idea is new to the person who has it. I then made a connection with the difficulty that some people have in perceiving the application for their work, or their private life for that matter, in what they do on management training courses. Some people find it difficult to learn because they cannot readily make the necessary connections. For them, whatever they are given to do away from work will be remote from it, literally and completely. If the examples and illustrations do not come from their own work situation, they are meaningless. The gap is too great to jump, or perhaps they would rather not realize that to learn anything worthwhile there has to be a gap.

It has been a lifelong mission in me to help people learn, starting with myself of course. Exploiting patterns is at the core of it, the meeting point of the two Thunks Distinguish and Symbolise that most closely reflect what I am calling conceptual in this context. It is a marriage of opposites, convergent/divergent, hard blue/soft green, you could almost say male/female. Whenever I need to make a point, to explain an idea, to persuade and enthuse I search for a model, a picture, an analogy to awaken in the other person or people an image of what is in my mind. It is by the process of putting thoughts into some coherent shape, into a pattern, that we communicate and learn.

Organizational Learning Styles

I now want to put forward two ideas for promoting organizational learning which look promising in the context of this book. One is about learning styles and the other about systems. Based on the work I have done with Thunks and the Thinking Intentions Profile (TIP) I have begun looking at how organizations think since I can build up a profile based on a composite of its individual members' styles. So far I have not covered more than limited parts of large organizations, so I cannot yet say how well such a composite picture would really reflect the whole of an organization's persona or culture. This kind of profiling however does seem to be helpful in recognizing the way that particular groups and departments try to get things done, what sorts of thing they will be likely to attempt, and how they learn to do it and learn from it. I am encouraged to carry on and see if our early beginnings over the past couple of years can be extrapolated to entire organizations. It seems reasonable to suppose that different divisions operating within the same business might have different approaches to thinking and learning.

If there were enough individual TIP profiles in our database to attempt to characterize several organizations it might be very instructive to compare their profiles, particularly to contrast competitors or businesses that were interested in one another for some other reason. People often ask me how the Shell profile compares with Esso. I do not have the TIP data required, but I would be willing to take a flying leap at a guess: Esso would be higher on the hard red and hard blue Thunks, while Shell would be higher on the soft red and soft blue. It remains to be seen. Naturally it would require the interest and the consent of those concerned in the exercise. But it is through experiment like this that people and organizations learn. Within an organization, it is already possible. I have on my database several hundreds from one company, Philips, Eindhoven, all of whom come from one function, namely Research and Development. The patterns thrown up by analysis of all these scores are of real interest in Philips. Possibly even more so if we have similar numbers of the R & D function in certain other companies, but that would require mutual collaboration of the companies concerned. The data are confidential.

I have chosen the R & D population to look at here to illustrate another possibility. Scientists give us an insight into how to improve organizational learning. For the very essence of what R & D people do is to learn. This is not an incidental aspect of their job, as with everyone else, but the very purpose of their work, its *raison d'être*. So how scientists go about learning is of special interest. It would be reasonable to assume that anything that has been carried on over many years, and with many successes, has established a deep body of knowledge about its operations. But this is not always true, and certainly not for R & D. Most large manufacturing businesses would give a lot to know more about 'developmentology' or whatever they would have to call the process of invention and innovation of new products. How can such a thing as invention be made 'efficient'? How can the time between conceiving some need and getting a new product into the market be shortened? How can viable ideas be produced on demand, and how can it be judged soon enough how viable they are going to be?

The scientists themselves do not know enough about how they work. They are by definition excellent thinkers, but often more focused on *what* they are trying to learn than *how*. Of course technical invention is only part of their process for achieving results. The range and variety of their activities is far greater than might be supposed. And R & D people themselves come in all shapes and sizes, even in the ways they use their minds. For some years now analysis of the development process itself has been going forward in Philips. Most of this is being done by the scientists themselves on their own work. They have been looking to see what is in common between them and where lie the differences in their development processes, not least, what ought to be changed. Alongside this analysis they have been identifying the distinct roles they actually undertake. Meanwhile, I have been profiling all those involved so that they can compare their roles with their individual thinking styles. The way is now open not only to picking 'horses for courses', but to recognizing what each scientist needs from others in his group, what kinds of support and what behaviour from colleagues will bring out his strengths. It is possible to predict his interactions with certain aspects of his work, or certain people with whom he doesn't readily get on. There is a chance of getting the best from the individual scientist and the working group, so that he can better manage himself and his work.

TIP is not restricted only to the cerebral aspect of thinking, but embraces also the influence of emotion and feelings, the senses, imagination and the spirit. The profile therefore has something to say about all of a scientist's work. How he observes and listens and communicates, how he tests judgements and makes decisions, how he influences people, how he handles ideas and learns. The value of using TIP to analyse thinking is that the Thunks and colour-frame can be used as well so that the person and his work are mapped in the same language. By this mapping on to a constant reference, it is possible to gain insights into the R & D process, enough to see how the process itself might be improved. For a few years now, this is what the scientists themselves have been doing, mapping their processes, exploring improvements and improving themselves.

The purpose of the profiling is not to fix the scientists in their style but to give them a way of framing themselves in conjunction with their work, and to go on framing and reframing as they learn and develop their understanding. For TIP is not primarily a tool for assessment, not a test of any kind, but an engine for development. You can see this engine pulling hard when you observe the scientists bent over their flow process diagrams or arguing with one another about how their work gets done. Since TIP is a preference inventory, it is possible for anyone to change his preferences, hence his profile and hence how he tackles his work. We know that some of the scientists do put effort into this and succeed in developing themselves. On the other hand, it is a real phenomenon that different scientists value different kinds of thinking processes differently, and that this can be deep and enduring. What matters is that each person knows this and also that he knows the differences between all his colleagues. Then everyone can get the best out of each other interpersonally.

Developing new products however is not simply an interpersonal transaction, though human communications are a significant aspect. There is the task to be done, and it will only be done well if addressed in particular ways. If a decision has to be made whether to stop a project, after many man-months of blood and tears have gone into it, then it's no use bringing to it the wrong parts of your mind. The same is true in principle for every task. With the colours and Thunks there is a language to recognize the mental operations of the task, the same as the language that describes mental intentions. It should be easier to match the two.

Like the R & D function, whole organizations have to learn all the time. And like the scientists they don't know how to do it. They are as much in need of good developmentology as the scientists themselves. From the work with the scientists, I can now see much more about how individuals prefer to tackle their work, and in this case, their thinking and learning work. I have a picture now of the variety of individual profiles doing comparable work, and also of the stress undergone when some of that work is not congenial. Because Thunks and colours contributed to the analysis of R & D roles and tasks, all those involved have learned more about the very function of development in a form that is amenable to making improvements. We have the prototype for doing the same thing in different departments, where the same principles would apply, however different the function might be. We have here a microcosm of a learning organization.

The Alliance of Systems and Training

My second idea for organizational learning is the active alliance of Training and Management Information Systems. These two functions are not normally associated, and yet in purpose they have much in common: the improvement of the operational effectiveness of all other departments. Equally, when taken separately, each function should supply results and services that are vital for the success of the other, but which at present widely go by default.

Let's put this idea in the context of different roles within the business, as I see them. In this instance, 'Director' is assigned to those who set the direction of the organization, regardless of title. Their role is to envision and determine its mission for the world it serves. Operational line functions such as R & D, Production, Sales and Distribution, are responsible for the main stream of getting things done. Functional specialist departments such as Marketing, Finance, Technical, Personnel, Public Affairs and Legal exist to execute and improve the performance of their own specific functions, through setting standards, expertise, influencing and offering services to the line. Both Systems and Training are normally seen in the last category, but I wish to single them out for a special role they share: they both scan all the other functions, line and staff. They are both of them creators, promoters and guardians of excellence. If one can say that the role of R & D is to learn, one could in a special sense say that the role of both Systems and Training is to teach. The responsibility for defining excellence through the establishing of directions and goals is of course with the organization's directors. These are the people who have the ultimate responsibility for excellence. It is they who have delegated to Systems and Training whatever role they have.

What I am calling 'Systems' may be found under various names: Management Services or Administration, Information Technology or Data Processing, Communications or even Finance. The same thing might be called Support Services in one business and Organization and Efficiency (O & E) in another. Whatever form it takes, the function has an increasingly high profile today. When the directors want to bring about significant change they look first to the mainstream line management. When they foresee complexity or difficulty they should turn to both Training and Systems, especially when they need something both rapid and enduring. I see Systems and Training as important engines of change within the organization. They are so complementary that the scope for synergy between them is just asking for an alliance. But evidently this is not so obvious, for otherwise it would be found everywhere. It might be easier to see how different their functions are than to realize how much they could do together. I hope that by comparing them in a rather unorthodox way, my point will be made.

Training is used here as the umbrella word for purposeful development of human performance when this is done off the job. Training has no role other than the improvement of other people's performance. The proper responsibility of every manager is to develop his own staff day by day. However he delegates some of it to Training, who can devote more specialized attention outside operating conditions. Learning done outside normal operating conditions has significant advantages. There is no risk and cost of making mistakes. The best available resources can be mustered for the 'teaching' end of it, people either inside or outside the company who are better for this specific purpose than the 'boss'. What has to be learned is distilled from all sources of best experience and received wisdom. Because of this concentration, training time is short. Learning time is reduced even further by focusing on only those peak experiences judged to be necessary for learning.

When training is of high quality and directed towards the authentic needs of the enterprise, it is one of the most cost-effective activities it undertakes. Whether calculable or not, the return on time and resources used ought to be a few hundred per cent. A first class investment. When I see a business in trouble cutting training, I know they are either in a cash-flow problem or they do not think their training brings such a competitive return. I would like to wave aside the issues about evaluation of the profit and other effects of training, because proper evaluation is costly, difficult and hardly ever attempted. More's the pity. Some training managers do not have the time and perhaps others would not dare. If more training managers were to go out into the field and listen and observe, they might be amazed at how much people have really taken on board.

It is only in badly managed organizations that Training is seen as a poor relation to its other main functions. The nature of the activity at its best makes it one of the toughest I know. Running a management development course demands continuous peak performance of such intensity that to do so too often is seriously damaging to health. Too many young trainers and developers are pushed to undertake workloads that involve face-to-face programmes week after week which drains their creative energy thus weakening their input to the development process and to follow-through in the field. Many years of my working life have been dedicated to improving performance through training, and developing managers is still a big part of my consultancy business. When I worked with Kepner Tregoe there was a company rule that no one should spend more than three weeks on the trot running programmes and that not often. It is a rule that I have continued to observe and advise others to follow if the high value added of training is to be maintained by those who deliver it.

But the irony or paradox is that training is too efficient to realize its potential for being effective. More and more ambitious goals are attempted in less and less time, so that the results of the compression are too rich to be taken in well. What has been distilled with enormous effort into a pill of concentrated experience needs to be dissolved into work in many ways over a long time for it to flow effectively into the bloodstream. I have been as guilty as anyone in striving to deliver a ton of value in an ounce of time. Moreover I have made serious attempts at the evaluation of results. This is why I am convinced they could be multiplied with a little help from Systems.

What is the role of Systems that I propose? First, any change that directors wish to bring about these days needs to spread through the whole organization and enter its bloodflow of normal operating conditions as quickly as possible. Systems is the ideal function for doing this, because systems designed deliberately by the Management Services function represent a more or less conscious effort to create the central nervous system of the corporate body. The growth of Information Technology provides a network of information flow that Systems can capitalize on to override the old structures of authority and hierarchy. This has been demonstrated most dramatically by those businesses that have made the needs of the customer paramount, and reorganized their communication channels accordingly. The information flowing through those channels has enormous energy of course and gives the system its force and power.

Systems represent a powerful way in which an organization 'teaches' those who use the system. Moreover while training is short and sharp, systems are enduring. While with training it is hard to reach a large number of people except over a long period, often absurdly over many years, systems affect everyone simultaneously. It is difficult to alter the inner habits of a lifetime during a short period off the job; much easier to exercise a steady and increasing influence on everyone through systems that by their nature bring uniformity, consistency, reliability and constancy. Systems are pervasive and enduring teachers.

Systems actually design work. Like tools, they amplify the power of their users. Computer systems, by causing information to be put into a form suitable for a machine, make human minds work in an 'efficient' way. Alongside the informal systems, they act like the laws of physics, or like one's habits, influencing the people involved whether they plan it or not. It seems plain that Systems has as much right as Training to be regarded as the 'teaching engine' of the learning organization. To make an overt and explicit alliance of the two would be even more valuable. Each can support and make up for the other. Systems needs the human element of Training and Training needs the machine element of Systems. One role of Training is the communication of difficult messages whether it be from top management or from Systems. The function can be used as a mediator, as a medium, that enables messages to go across functional boundaries. User Interface Design is notoriously difficult: Training can ease the difficulty, especially because it is concerned with social, interactive processes between people in a way that is not typically found in Systems people themselves. It is little use however trying to improve performance via Training if the changes in approach being promoted either cut across or are not supported by ongoing systems.

There will always be ongoing systems that carry the mainstream processes of the business, like a sales order system, a despatch system, an accounting system, marketing and production systems and so on. Such systems and procedures represent the rules or ideal methods of the enterprise, that show people how they should carry out specific tasks. If Training does not cross-reference the changes it is promoting with ongoing systems, then energy will be burned up in friction, conflict and despair. Both Training and Systems should automatically look to one another with the basic question, 'Who else will be affected by what I do?' And even better, 'Who else could help with what I do?'

If the organization's brain needs systems, the human brain needs maps and tools. Many people have their own personal systems for encouraging themselves to operate effectively, and in a way the maps and other tools mentioned in this book offer ideas to adapt and adopt for this purpose. When such tools are used often enough to be grooved in, they become habits, which is the human version of systems. I used the word 'human' on purpose. For it feels natural to see a system more like a machine than a person, with more hard structure than soft motive and feeling. There is a real sense that systems are hostile to man and cage him in to relevance, so that people either despise, ignore or reject them, in the name of human freedom. Yet we need the discipline and the frameworks to enable our freedom to flourish. One of the yardsticks I have used for years to give me a feel for the results of training is the extent to which people go back to their work and change an operating system or design a new one. They often do. When this happens, and it works better, then instead of fading after the course, something they had 'learned' is actually increased in the months following it. After that, there's no looking back for them.

What a chance there is for consciously designing into this nervous system the conceptual tools that would direct and promote the effectiveness of everyone who worked with them. Because they are all-pervasive and continuous, commanding the arteries of the business, Systems could have much more effect on learning than the intensely concentrated periods within which most training events are constrained. It is possible, then, for the organization to be 'a machine for learning in'. Maps and other tools can be used purposefully to improve the learning curve of both individuals and the structures within which they work. Awareness of the learning process can make all work self-improving, as well as raising the potential of those concerned.

The strongest possible bridge between these unlikely bedfellows, Systems and Training, is when whatever is being offered is generic. The very concept of 'generic' is the keystone to the bridge. Then it should apply and be applied system-wide. It will work universally. It will help the review of systems themselves, and then cross all boundaries of function and discipline. This is why a common language of thought is useful. If Systems and Training could work more closely together, they could use one another's distinctive strengths and make up for the respective weaknesses. Training is good for sowing seeds, for start-ups and acceleration. It gets people excited and moved. Insights are sometimes reached which affect behaviour for a lifetime. It is the most efficient use of time in bringing about a change of heart. Systems have silent organizational power, and they are more reliable in changing behaviour, especially if designed in support of training. Since both are simply the agents of those who set and manage the direction of the business, surely they should work hand in hand?

Afterword

This book has been written not for the average manager of the past but for the better manager of the future. Yet this does not mean losing sight of all that is known about the very best of managers past and present. Three of the hallmarks of the super manager are a sense of the market, handling people well, and conceptual power. In the first instance he is a practical realist, aware of his surroundings, his streetwise instincts sharply tuned; and he has a sort of future feel, a way of reaching out and experiencing the future before it comes. Second, he will have got where he is with the help of other people, so he must be doing a lot of things right when it comes to empathy, warmth and love; he leads by getting others to follow, collaborate and push him there. Third, he can use his mind well; he forms useful patterns and connections between events, is analytical and logical, seems to ask the right questions and use the answers to recognize what is still missing; and yet has the mental flexibility to handle the unexpected and the imagination to invite it. The first two characteristics, market future feel and handling people well, each has something special about it. But both are heavily influenced by the third and this is why it is in the conceptual area I have focused this book and my work with managers over the past twenty years.

Success attends those who actually do what they intend. They match their actions with their goals, their deeds with their thoughts. While this is obvious at first sight, it turns out to be extraordinarily difficult to accomplish. Most people don't, and end up shooting themselves in the foot. Their energy is dissipated or even so misdirected as to actively prevent their achieving what they want, even when they would have been able to do so. The reasons for this are all to do with getting one's act together, managing conflicting aspects in the most practical way. In concluding this book I want to highlight some key points which may not otherwise come through.

Intentionality itself is one of the problems. It is in practice quite wrong to assume that anyone is fully aware of his own intention. Intention is an extremely complex animal, requiring no little skill to unravel and identify, even in oneself. Goals are situational values, the sharp end of intention, which are constantly being brought into focus by the desire to face up to a particular situation. Values operate more or less below the surface continuously, and those that are unchanging represent the very nature of a person, the basis of his approach to life. When a particular goal or criterion is taken up and put to work, it will invariably be because of some reason underlying it, and also because it is seen as likely to fulfil some other purpose beyond it. The potential complexity is horrendous and usually not pursued, with fatal results. For it is the values we are not aware of that may invisibly give us the most trouble, for they are actually influencing our thinking at a deep level without our being able to manage their effect on us. Everyone becomes painfully aware of it when his own values conflict with one another because this is what requires him to make a decision, to reconcile the conflict. Likewise we are all too often brought up against the different values of other people, and can at least try to manage that. What we cannot manage are the values and goals that do not surface visibly, that often form the main drive of our intention. Getting through to genuine intention requires conceptual skill and conceptual tools to help it happen.

Intention is by its nature 'inner' and needs to be brought out on to the table in the outer world. It is also essentially abstract and hence obscure and difficult; this makes it vital to make values concrete, to spell them out in the form of concrete and recognizable options or threats or events or activities, so as to observe their effect and thereby know what they are. That is why the estate agent shows new customers lots of houses so as to observe their reaction and thus deduce their objectives, which are more abstract. Usually people muddle up one with the other being unable to recognize the difference between an objective and an option, a fear and a threat. It is of critical importance to have a sound conceptual framework and discipline within which to juggle different kinds of thought. Without it, a person will actually reject what is in his own best interests or embrace something that will not achieve what he really intends. It can often be true that to achieve a goal is easier than to know what it is or should be.

An even more obvious reason for failure to do what one intends is because one can't. To say that this means the person is not able to is to state only one side of the equation, which indeed might be difficult to change overnight. The other side of the equation is how it might be done, or how else. This means coming up with ideas that were not obvious when the intention was seen as impossible to achieve. Many people fail even to look for further ideas, alternative ways to do it.

Awareness is so often inadequate. To start with, we clearly cannot ever expect to be aware of all the possible ideas that might be useful in any particular situation: the successfulness of using imagination can hardly be guaranteed. Yet although the unusual and excellent idea needed might remain elusive and never be found, at least it can be ensured that someone goes out and looks for ideas when they need to, and will also give a welcome to any ideas and suggestions offered. Though the nature of imagination seems at first to be totally averse to analysis, it is actually the case that tools have been found that increase the probability of reaching an idea. To find such tools requires many years of conceptualizing and testing, so that it can be demonstrated that the notion of a creative tool or instrument is not actually a contradiction in terms. Obviously we cannot exercise our will over ideas we cannot even conceive.

To adapt a phrase, where there is imagination there is a way. If this is not sought no wonder that someone fails to realize his intention. No one can do something if he hasn't even thought it up.

In my experience people who are exceptionally resourceful with ideas are in a minority. The way they handle information is often alien to the majority and indeed very imaginative people can be severely misunderstood and at worst even rejected by the tribe when they seem too far out. This makes it important to be able to recognize when a task needs an imaginative attack, as distinct from one demanding relevance, whether driven by reason or by feelings. And it explains why special kinds of structure are often helpful in promoting creative thinking. Some structural tools act like frameworks of discipline which justify total freedom within their safe bounds; others drive thinking outwards and beyond the normal, overtly and explicitly searching for the unusual and out of reach ideas. Unless someone has allowed the unusual to be considered, his choice of action can never be really free.

Awareness of both values and possible actions is thus essential for actually doing what one actually wants. By his recognition and involvement, Man creates the situations that open up around him: he is therefore the key to their solution. The dissatisfaction that calls for action stems either from failures in his own performance or from setting his goals too high. Awareness of self is therefore as important as awareness of the surrounding world. He needs to manage the forces both within and outside his own boundary, and maintain a balance that is aptly alert and harmonious. No one can truly exercise free will unless he is aware of his values, has at least tried to search for options beyond the obvious, and has information about those options in terms of his values that is something approaching reality. Furthermore, he needs some disciplined structure that is entirely objective, so as to ensure that his reason is exercised appropriately. Without both awareness and reason, his will cannot have a chance to be free.

Competence is the other factor I want to conclude with here. It is possible to be clear about goals, have thought up an idea that might work and yet be unable to put things together. It is all too common for people to know something and yet fail to use their information well. If this is due to pressure of time all the more reason for being efficient. Thinking is an activity to avoid doing what would be useless, costly or dangerous. It is pretending to do instead of actually doing. Those who refuse to think are forced to work too hard to make up for it; those who are wise not only invest in thinking but, to avoid working with their bare hands mentally speaking, make conceptual tools to help. There are very few tasks where thinking will not save time and improve results, both. Abstraction is a short cut to action.

When it comes to competences, I believe that much of the effort currently being expended on establishing core management competences is missing the big point. Only a fool would call an ability to use a computer a core management competence: that is obviously still too peripheral. By core competence we usually mean some kind of sufficiency which is central, which commands the whole area of expertise from the heights. Yet some so called competences of management seem very peripheral indeed when compared with the competence of thinking.

Amid constant change, where a manager is meeting so many situations for the first time ever, he needs to have at least part of any new task already familiar to him. His tools are the familiar part. It is their tools that enable consultants to be useful even when they have no experience of the situation they are asked to face. More and more managers will also want a set of tools they can trust and hang on to. What is really wanted are tools or competences that will not get out of date and so are stable and unchanging; tools that are required and used very often; that apply to most activities; and above all tools that are fundamental to all results. Tools and competences need to be universal and eternal, in short generic and few. Having only a few tools engenders increasing competence in their user and because they apply to all other aspects of expertise they contribute to that general competence that is required to exploit the more specific know-how.

With great diversity and change around us we must deploy all the advantages learned over the centuries, based on the essential unity of knowledge. Generic laws are not limited to physics, mathematics or music. The purpose of all teaching is to help someone do something better or more easily, the same purpose it shares with the tool. The point of all learning is to find those tools that will make things easier. I hope this book will encourage you to be a toolmaker for yourself. And thus to make it more possible to realize your intentions, to do what you actually want, perhaps even what you actually need.